Returns in Over-the-Counter Stock Markets

Returns in Over-the-Counter Stock Markets

PAUL F. JESSUP and ROGER B. UPSON

UNIVERSITY OF MINNESOTA PRESS

Minneapolis

© Copyright 1973 by the University of Minnesota.
All rights reserved.
Printed in the United States of America
at Lund Press, Minneapolis
Published in the United Kingdom and India by the
Oxford University Press, London and Delhi, and in
Canada by the Copp Clark Publishing Co.
Limited, Toronto

Library of Congress Catalog Card Number: 73-77711

ISBN 0-8166-0690-0

Preface

EXTENSIVE NEW INFORMATION about over-the-counter stock markets is presented and analyzed in this book, which is designed for individual investors, professional portfolio managers, and public officials concerned with securities markets.

Individual investors have included over-the-counter (OTC) stocks in their portfolios for many years. More recently, institutions, which generally had confined their stock holdings to listed shares and some widely held over-the-counter stocks, have become more active investors in OTC stocks of smaller, newer companies. Such institutions include mutual funds, bank trust departments, insurance companies, pension funds, and endowment funds. Thus, the public, both directly as investors and indirectly as beneficiaries of institutional portfolios, has increased its participation in OTC markets in recent years.

Despite greater public participation, information about OTC markets is incomplete. Books about securities markets principally describe the mechanics of the New York Stock Exchange (NYSE), and to a minor extent they discuss operating characteristics of the OTC market network. Recent research in securities markets focuses mainly on stocks listed on the NYSE.

A basic need in financial literature is filled by this book. Instead of de-

v

scribing the mechanism for buying and selling OTC shares and the regulatory environment of OTC markets, this book examines returns from various OTC markets over an extended time period, 1946–69. It analyzes the national OTC market, made up of widely held stocks of relatively large firms, and also regional OTC markets centered in five metropolitan areas:

Atlanta
Chicago
Minneapolis-St. Paul
St. Louis
San Francisco

The principal questions dealt with in this study include the following:

What are the dimensions of OTC markets?
What are investment returns in various OTC markets?
What is the impact of portfolio diversification in these markets?
How volatile are returns from OTC markets?

Throughout the book these questions are approached from an investor's point of view.

Many investors should find this book valuable. It provides a counterweight to selected case examples of OTC stocks that have successfully risen from obscurity to provide substantial long-run investment returns. Success stories concerning OTC stocks often are well publicized. In contrast, investors with high expectations have purchased shares of OTC companies that eventually became valueless. These adverse investment outcomes tend to be quickly forgotten except by those who encountered substantial losses. By avoiding selected examples and instead analyzing portfolio outcomes, this book provides investors with information for testing their expectations about future returns from portfolios of OTC stocks. These OTC expectations can then be related to alternative investment opportunities.

Public policy, both at federal and state levels, is increasingly becoming involved with OTC markets. The Securities and Exchange Commission now demands broader disclosure by many companies that have shares traded in OTC markets. The Federal Reserve System has extended margin requirements to encompass selected OTC stocks. In various states, laws and regulations relating to OTC markets are being reexamined and

Preface

revised. Also, increasing participation by institutional investors in OTC stocks is receiving the attention of federal and state regulatory officials. In this environment of reexamination and change, this analysis of OTC markets provides an important foundation for research studies and for public-policy decisions concerning securities laws and investment regulations.

PFJ
RBU

Acknowledgments

ASSISTING US in collecting and verifying the information for this study were the following individuals: Garry Barnett, Stuart Curet, Marvin Geisness, Carmencita Hernandez, Roger King, Thomas Medcalf, Donald Mingo, Ford Pearson, Patricia Schempp, Michael Smith, Linda Stang, and John Timmer.

Individuals providing us with important computer programming support were David Holland, Richard Johnson, and Per Mokkelbost. Statistical assistance was provided by Keishiro Matsumoto and Per Mokkelbost.

Funding for part of this project was from research grants from the Graduate School of Business Administration, University of Minnesota. In addition, computer time was made available to us through grants from the University Computer Center. Typing of the several drafts of this manuscript was done by various secretaries of the Department of Finance and Insurance.

Helping us to achieve an improved final manuscript were our colleagues W. Bruce Erickson and Ronald Christner, the anonymous reviewers of the University of Minnesota Press, and the staff of the Press.

Any errors of commission or omission remain our responsibility.

From development to completion, this joint research project incurred much of our time and consideration. We acknowledge the cheerful devotion of our wives and families.

PFJ
RBU

ix

Contents

Figures

Tables

PART I. Identifying Over-the-Counter Markets

1 Over-the-Counter Market Systems: An Introduction

THIS CHAPTER SPECIFIES interrelationships and dimensions of over-the-counter (OTC) markets, both at a point in time and as a process over time. It does not provide detailed descriptions of each of these markets.

Framework

Over-the-counter markets, which include both a national and diverse regional markets, constitute one sector of the nation's securities markets. Although bonds, warrants, and other financial instruments are traded in some of these markets, only common stocks are analyzed in this book.

The registered exchanges, such as the American Stock Exchange and the New York Stock Exchange, make up the other sector of the securities markets. The exchanges are registered with the Securities and Exchange Commission under provisions of the Securities Exchange Act of 1934. Each exchange is a centralized marketplace where listed securities can be bought and sold by members for their own account or as agents for nonmembers. By meeting specific criteria relating principally to corporate size, history, and breadth of ownership, a company can become eligible for listing its securities on one or more of these exchanges. In addition, in seeking listing for its shares, a company's management must agree to pro-

3

vide timely public disclosure of accounting statements, dividend declarations, and other material information.

The New York Stock Exchange (NYSE) is the principal registered exchange, as measured by the aggregate market value of common stocks listed on it. Also, since it lists the common shares of most of the nation's large, widely owned companies, the NYSE has long been a focal point of investor interest and participation. Information is readily available about the structure and operations of the NYSE and about companies that have shares listed on it. Similarly most recent investment studies are limited to shares traded on the NYSE. Nevertheless, the NYSE is but one of the nation's stock markets.

In contrast to the registered exchanges, the nation's over-the-counter markets are less structured systems. Shares of many publicly owned corporations not listed on one of the registered exchanges are traded over the counter. To be eligible for OTC trading, shares need not meet all the requirements for listing on various registered exchanges, but only certain basic requirements of federal and state securities laws. There is no centralized marketplace for OTC stocks; rather transactions are conducted by communication among dealers in diverse locations.[1] The structure and interrelationships of various OTC markets at a point in time are shown in Figure 1-1.

Since this book focuses on investor experience, the various OTC markets are categorized on the basis of information generally available to investors. Such information is publicized regularly in the *Wall Street Journal* and the financial sections of major metropolitan newspapers. Over-the-counter market quotations also appear in other, more specialized, financial publications, such as the daily quotation sheets distributed by the National Quotation Bureau, but these data are not readily available to many investors.

A set of unlisted stocks, judged to have widespread investor and dealer interest by a committee of the National Association of Securities Dealers (NASD), is reported regularly in the *Wall Street Journal*. As can be seen in Figure 1-1, these stocks constitute the national OTC market. Relative to the national list, another set of OTC stocks is judged by a NASD committee to be less widely held. This category of stocks is published weekly

1. Currently a computerized information system about selected OTC stocks is being developed. Its title is the National Association of Securities Dealers Automated Quotation system (NASDAQ).

in the *Wall Street Journal*, and as depicted in Figure 1-1, it does not overlap with the national group.

Regional OTC markets exist in many metropolitan areas. Major newspapers of these areas provide quotations of OTC stocks judged by a regional committee of the NASD to be of particular interest to investors and dealers of the region. Often these are shares of companies with local headquarters or other facilities. Some of these companies are small, localized operations while others, although based locally, have widespread operations and extensive investor and dealer interest. In the latter case, the shares are likely to appear in the national OTC market. Figure 1-1 illustrates that the various regional OTC markets do not overlap with the national OTC market. However, there is overlap among regional OTC shares and the weekly OTC category.

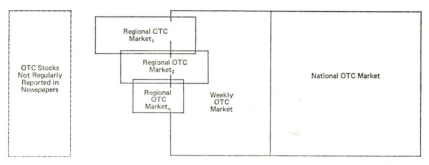

Figure 1-1. Conceptualization of OTC stock markets at a point in time

Shares of many other companies are neither listed on any registered exchange nor quoted regularly in generally available financial news sources. They are represented by the dotted box in Figure 1-1. This lack of regular quotation implies that these shares are of companies with relatively few shareholders and limited investor interest. In some cases the companies may be rather large, but the shares are closely held and inactively traded. To illustrate, almost every one of the country's approximately 13,000 banks is a corporation. However, only a small percentage of these institutions have their shares regularly quoted in major daily newspapers. Similarly, for shares of some nonbanking companies there is no publicized market; rather a company's officers may introduce potential buyers and sellers. Such lack of information precludes effective measurement of the magnitude of this set of stocks. Therefore, while recognizing the existence of an "inactive market" for OTC stocks, this book focuses only on OTC markets that receive regular financial coverage in principal newspapers.

Whereas Figure 1-1 conceptualizes OTC markets at a point in time, Figure 1-2 shows the transition process in market quotation that may be experienced by a common stock. The solid lines indicate directional changes in market quotation that reflect a broadening market for a company's stock. For instance, initially the shares of a small new company may be quoted in a regional OTC market. This implies that the shares principally are of interest to local investors and dealers. If the company's operations grow successfully, the shares are likely to attract more investors and dealers so that at a later point in time a NASD committee will classify the stock in the national OTC market. Subsequently the company's operating and financial success and its broadened distribution of shareholders may enable it to meet the listing criteria of a registered exchange. To illustrate such a transition process, during 1958–60 price quotations for shares of Control Data Corporation were reported in the Minneapolis-St. Paul regional OTC market; from 1960 to 1963 the shares were included in the National OTC quotations of the *Wall Street Journal*; beginning in 1963 the shares were listed on the NYSE.

Mergers may broaden the market for a company's shares. For example, a company that has shares trading in a regional OTC market may merge

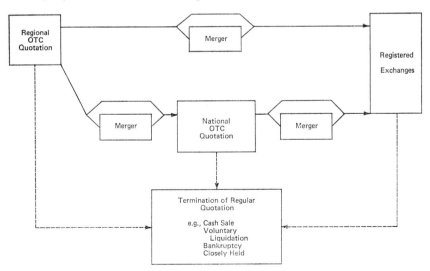

Figure 1-2. Transition paths of market listings of OTC stocks

6

with a company whose shares are traded in the national OTC market or on the NYSE. Although the regional market quotation is terminated by the merger, an investor who exchanges his shares for those of the acquiring company then holds shares trading in a broader market. For this reason, Figure 1-2 illustrates merger as a possible route to a broader market.

The dashed lines in Figure 1-2 show transitions where quotations for a stock cease to be regularly available. Stocks can cease to be quoted because of cash merger, liquidation, bankruptcy, or acquisition by a closely held company. Other stocks may move into the "not regularly quoted" category if they become closely held or the company lapses into relative inactivity. Figure 1-2 also indicates that a stock may stay in the same market over time, in which case it remains in one of the rectangles and does not follow any of the transition paths.

Market Specification

This study examines the national OTC market and the regional OTC markets in Atlanta, Chicago, Minneapolis-St. Paul, St. Louis, and San Francisco. These five were chosen because of their being identified with regional financial centers (each having a Federal Reserve Bank), their geographic diversity, and the availability of stock price quotations from these markets.

The basic time period of this study is 1946–69. Nineteen forty-six was the first year after the end of World War II, and 1969 was the most recent complete year that could be included in this study.[2] This twenty-four-year time span provides a long-run perspective on OTC markets, and it encompasses periods of both generally rising and falling stock prices.

For each market, the total number of quoted stocks (i.e., the population) is enumerated at the beginning of each year.[3] This procedure is necessary because markets change over time. The industrial composition of companies having stocks traded over the counter reflects the changing importance of various industries in the nation's economy. For example, during the postwar period, electronics and computer firms make up a

2. Data for this study were collected during 1970–71.

3. Until recently shares of two major types of business, banks and insurance companies, were not listed on the NYSE but were traded almost exclusively in OTC markets. Because an objective of this study is to compare returns of OTC stocks with those of NYSE stocks, it was decided to *exclude* bank and insurance shares from the defined OTC market.

7

changing proportion of OTC stocks. From the enumerated populations are drawn random samples of thirty stocks, at yearly intervals.

For the national OTC market, the first issue each year of the *Wall Street Journal* is used to define the population of available stocks. The first random sample is drawn from the issue of January 2, 1946, and additional samples are drawn at the beginning of each year through 1969.

For the regional OTC markets, principal daily newspapers of these areas contain quotations of stocks as provided by regional committees of the NASD. In the *Minneapolis Tribune*, OTC quotations are separated into "national" and "local" sections. In the *Atlanta Constitution*, the *Chicago Daily News*, the *St. Louis Post-Dispatch*, and the *San Francisco Chronicle*, the OTC stock quotations are in one list. However, these lists include some stocks that also appear daily in the *Wall Street Journal*'s national OTC list, and so for this study such stocks in the national population are excluded from the regional populations. For these regional markets, the first random sample is drawn at the beginning of 1955, except for St. Louis, for which price quotations first became available for the 1956 sample. Resource constraints prevented collection of regional data back to 1946.

For each market a data bank is constructed comprising such information on each sampled stock as cash distributions, capital changes, and prices. Information regarding the yearly cash distribution of each stock includes all cash dividends, regular as well as extra, and cash-equivalent distributions such as the market value of any rights or spin-offs distributed to shareholders.

Capital changes include stock dividends, stock splits, and changes arising from merger or reorganization. In these cases, an investor's holdings of a company's shares change. Such capital changes are explicitly included in this study.[4]

Prices are the reported bid and asked quotation for a stock at the end of the year. Whereas the year-end closing price of a stock listed on a registered exchange is usually that of the year's last actual sale, the year-end quotation for an OTC stock is reported on the basis of a bid and asked price. For example, an OTC stock may be quoted at 15 bid, 15½ asked. Basically, at a point in time, the bid is the price at which a dealer is willing to buy stock from a holder, and the asked is a higher price at which a dealer is willing to sell stock to a potential purchaser.

4. For an explanation of computational procedures, see Chapter 2.

Because actual transactions are not reported during the time period of this study, bid and asked quotations provide the only historical price series for OTC stocks. The various NASD committees state that the prices are indicative of those at which transactions could have been made. These prices are used by portfolio managers and regulatory agencies to value holdings of OTC stocks. Reliability of OTC price quotations is regularly monitored by self-regulatory committees of the securities industry and by the Securities and Exchange Commission. Occasional misquotations in data sources are possible, but such reporting errors can be assumed to be random.[5]

The difference between the bid and asked prices at a point in time is called the spread. To measure investor experience, it is postulated in this study that stocks are purchased at the asked price (the price at which a dealer offers shares) and then valued at subsequent bid prices. To illustrate, at the beginning of 1962 the shares of Control Data Corporation were quoted in the national OTC market at $39½ bid, $42 asked. At the beginning of 1963, these shares were quoted at $31¼ bid, $33¼ asked. Therefore in this study, shares purchased at $42 at the beginning of 1962 are valued at $31¼ at the beginning of 1963. This procedure, which provides for transaction costs, is critically evaluated in Chapter 3.[6]

The final step in market specification is an assessment of the accuracy of each market's data bank. A random sample of stocks was drawn from each data bank, and information about these stocks was independently collected. When these independent audit data were compared with the initial information, no consistent errors were found. Random errors, which were infrequent and minor, were corrected. In sum, the collection and verification procedures assure that there is a high degree of accuracy.

Market Dimensions

The number of common stocks in the national OTC market has been increasing more rapidly than that on the New York Stock Exchange.

5. For more detail about the quality and mechanics of OTC quotations, see Leo M. Loll, Jr., and Julian E. Buckley, *The Over-the-Counter Securities Markets: A Review Guide*, 2nd ed. (Englewood Cliffs, N.J.: Prentice-Hall, Inc., 1967), Chapter 11.

6. Until 1965–66, published price quotations for OTC stocks included a retail markup and/or commission.

Returns in OTC Stock Markets

From 1946 to 1970 the number of national OTC common stocks reported daily in the *Wall Street Journal* increased approximately 550 percent. During the same time span the number of common stocks listed on the NYSE increased 48 percent. While the increase in OTC quotations must be viewed in relation to its smaller base, the growth was such that by 1970 the reported number of national OTC stocks was close to that of the NYSE. (Table 1-1.)

Table 1-1. Number of Common Stocks Listed on the NYSE or Reported in the National OTC Market for Selected Years, 1946–70 (as of January 1)

Market	1946	1950	1955	1960	1965	1970
New York Stock Exchange[a]	881	1039	1076	1092	1227	1290
National OTC Stock Market[b]	170	396	446	357[c]	942	1123

[a] As reported in *New York Stock Exchange Fact Book*, 1971, p. 78.

[b] As explained in the text, these figures are derived from the *Wall Street Journal.* Bank and insurance stocks are excluded.

[c] This figure does not include stocks listed in the Eastern edition of the *Wall Street Journal.* (See text.)

The relatively large increase in national OTC stocks may reflect a combination of factors, such as: (1) a net increase in companies with publicly traded shares; (2) increased investor interest in corporate shares that were previously inactively traded; and (3) geographically broadened financial reporting of OTC shares.

The increased number of national OTC stocks also reflects changes in definitional criteria and reporting coverage. From 1946 until 1956 the *Wall Street Journal* contained an "Over-the-Counter Market" list, regularly and conveniently available to nationwide readers. In November 1956, the newspaper began dividing OTC stocks into various lists. One was a "National Market" which appeared in all the newspaper's regional editions, and the others were separate listings for each regional edition — Eastern, Midwest, Pacific Coast, and Southwest. This dichotomy persisted through 1962. In January 1963, the different regional listings were discontinued, and a "revised and expanded list" of OTC quotations was introduced in all editions. The newspaper stated that "to bring more issues into nation-wide coverage," it was lowering "its requirement on the number of stockholders each stock in the daily list must have" from about 1500 to 1000. Also geographical criteria were revised. Thus, while the coverage of national OTC stocks was revised at least twice during 1946–

10

69, this study consistently defines "national OTC stocks" as only those having daily nationwide quotations in the *Wall Street Journal*.

In the five regional OTC markets analyzed in this study, the number of stocks generally increased during 1955–70. As presented in Table 1-2, the amount of growth varies, with the number of local OTC stocks reported in Atlanta declining during 1955–70. Furthermore, Table 1-2 indicates the variability of the number of stocks within each regional OTC market over time.

Table 1-2. Number of Common Stocks Reported in Five Regional OTC Markets for Selected Years, 1955–70 (as of January 1)[a]

Regional OTC Market	1955	1960	1965	1970
Atlanta	50	46	36	32
Chicago	42	108	51	55
Minneapolis-St. Paul	30	38	94	239
St. Louis	0	31	35	27
San Francisco	33	29	20	44
Total	155	252	236	397

[a] The criteria for defining these five regional OTC markets and the various data sources are discussed in the text. Bank and insurance stocks are excluded from the figures.

Occasionally a stock quoted in one regional OTC market is also quoted in another regional market. This is infrequent because a company's stock becomes a candidate for NASD reclassification from the "regional" to "national" category as it begins to attract geographically wider news coverage and investor interest. As confirmation of this process, a comparison of the stocks in each of the five regional markets shows only minor overlap. Thus, at a point in time, each regional market is basically autonomous in its component stocks.

Summary

National and regional OTC markets have not previously been subjects of comprehensive analysis. This omission is especially notable in view of their prevalence, growth, and interrelationships with other components of the nation's securities markets.

Therefore, to examine simulated investor experience in OTC markets, a data bank of prices, dividends, and capital changes was compiled for randomly selected OTC stocks traded nationally or in regional OTC markets centered in five principal financial centers. In total, selected data on over 500 nationally traded stocks and 700 regionally traded stocks were collected. This new information provides the basis for analyzing returns from various OTC markets, thus offering new insights for market partici-pants, researchers, and public-policy officials.

PART II. Measuring Market Returns

2 Indexes versus Rates of Return

INDEXES OF STOCK PRICES, computations of dividend yield, and comprehensive rates of return are widely used as measures of investor experience in securities markets. In this chapter, not only is a widely reported price index of OTC stocks shown to have major limitations, but new, more comprehensive measures are also introduced.

An OTC Market Index

Indexes are one way of summarizing numerically the performance of a stock market and various subcategories of stocks. To examine the past price history of the New York Stock Exchange, investors refer to such indexes as the Dow Jones Composite Average of sixty-five stocks, the Standard & Poor's 500 Stock Index, and, more recently, the New York Stock Exchange's own Composite Indicator. Other indexes, such as the Dow Jones Utility Average, principally summarize price histories of more narrowly defined subgroupings of NYSE stocks.

During the twenty-five-year time span of this study, there is only one regularly available and widely reported stock market index which contains solely OTC stocks.[1] This is the National Quotation Bureau (NQB) OTC

1. More comprehensive OTC indexes, derived from the NASDAQ system, were inaugurated in 1971.

Returns in OTC Stock Markets

Industrial Index, reported daily in the *Wall Street Journal* and some other newspapers. Although the index was begun in 1948, it has been computed back to 1938. The index comprises thirty-five stocks, none of which is listed on any registered stock exchange. The technical construction of the NQB Index is similar to that of the Dow Jones Averages in that the weight of a stock in the index is determined by its price.

The thirty-five stocks in the NQB Index of OTC stocks as of January 1, 1970, were as follows: [2]

Acme Visible	Kaiser Steel
Allyn & Bacon	Kearney & Trecker
American Express	Eli Lilly Co.
American Greetings	Magnetics, Inc.
Anheuser-Busch	Mallinckrodt Chemical
Arrow Hart	Works "A"
Barnes Hind	Midas International
Berkshire Hathaway	Nicholson File
Brockway Glass	A. C. Nielsen "B"
Brush Beryllium	Noxell Corp.
Buckbee Mears Co.	Raychem
Cannon Mills	O. M. Scott
Computer Usage Co.	Tampax, Inc.
Economics Laboratory	Techumseh Products
Hexcel Corp.	Tidewater Marine Service
Hoover Co.	Trico Products
Hyster Co.	U.S. Envelope
Inland Container	U.S. Financial Corp.

Between the beginning of 1946 and the beginning of 1970, this OTC index value increased almost elevenfold.[3] An elevenfold increase in twenty-four years implies a compound increase in excess of 10 percent each year. Since the index is based solely on stock prices, this rate of increase does not allow for cash dividends.

The potential diversity of OTC markets and their component stocks may be incompletely summarized in the NQB Index. As discussed in the preceding chapter, there are diverse OTC markets made up of "national" and "regional" stocks.

2. *Over-the-Counter Securities Review*, January 1970, vol. 19, no. 7, issue 223, p. 4.

3. Estimated from data in Wilford J. Eiteman, Charles A. Dice, and David K. Eiteman, *The Stock Market*, 4th ed. (New York: McGraw-Hill, 1966), p. 196, and *Over-the-Counter Securities Review*, January 1970, p. 4.

Indexes versus Rates of Return

Figure 2-1 presents a frequency distribution of the component stocks of the NQB Index, classified by total market value of a firm's equity. In addition, Figure 2-1 portrays distributions of representative samples of national OTC and NYSE common stocks.

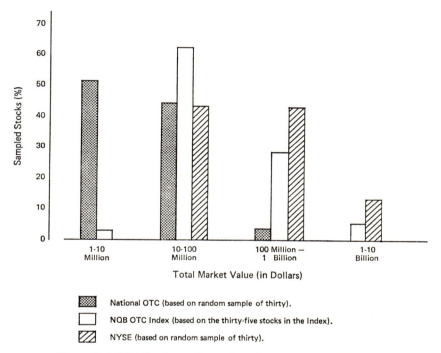

Figure 2-1. Distributions of samples of common stock by total market value of shares, January 1, 1970

The median market value is $155 million for the NYSE stocks, $76 million for the component stocks in the NQB Index, and $10 million for the national OTC stocks. Less than 3 percent of the stocks in the NQB Index are of firms whose total market value of equity is less than $10 million, while over 50 percent of the randomly selected national OTC stocks are in this size category. It is improbable that the stocks in the NQB Index as of January 1, 1970, could have been selected at random from the national OTC market.[4]

Stocks in the NQB Index also differ significantly from the representa-

4. Median-comparison test; 95 percent confidence level.

17

Returns in OTC Stock Markets

Table 2-1. Price and Dividend Characteristics of Samples
of Common Stocks Traded in Various Markets,
January 1, 1970

Category	Median Price as of January 1, 1970 (in Dollars)	Stocks Paying Cash Dividends in Preceding Year (%)
National OTC stocks[a]	7	28
NQB Index stocks	42	89
NYSE stocks[a]	28	93

[a] Based on random sample.

tive sample of national OTC stocks in share price and cash dividends paid.[5] Median price and cash dividend-payment characteristics are presented in Table 2-1. Indeed, in terms of per-share prices and cash dividend payments, the stocks in the NQB Index are more similar to NYSE stocks than to a random sample of national OTC stocks.

In summary, the NQB Index measures price changes of selected stocks of larger companies. This analysis of characteristics of the stocks in the NQB Index in January 1970 is consistent with an earlier description of this index: "The 35 stocks selected for the average are chosen from over-the-counter stocks with the largest market value, the largest number of stockholders, and the most substantial records."[6] Thus the composition of this index is limited, and a more comprehensive representation of OTC stocks is required.

Rate-of-Return Measures

Stock price indexes also fail to measure explicitly a shareholder's total return, for they focus only on the change in market prices of stocks over time. From the viewpoint of a shareholder, the rate of return received on a stock for a single year comprises two elements: the dividends and other cash-equivalent distributions received; and the per-share change in the value of the stock. Both elements must be adjusted for possible capital changes, such as a stock split.

Conceptually the one-year, rate-of-return formulation is as follows:[7]

5. Median-comparison test and binomial test; 95 percent confidence level.

6. Eiteman, Dice, and Eiteman, *The Stock Market*, p. 195.

7. This is the internal rate of return for one year. Longer holding-period returns also are computed using internal rate of return.

18

Indexes versus Rates of Return

$$\text{RoR} = \left[\frac{D + (P_2 - P_1)}{P_1}\right] \times 100$$

Where:

RoR = Rate of return, expressed as a percentage.
D = Total cash dividends received during the year.
P_2 = End-of-year price per share.
P_1 = Beginning-of-year price per share.

The figures above are appropriately adjusted for stock splits and cash-equivalent distributions (such as rights with a market value).

For example, assume that at the beginning of a year an investor purchases a share of stock for $20 ($P_1 = 20$), that during the year he receives $1 in cash dividends ($D = 1$), and that at the end of the year the share of stock is priced at $22 ($P_2 = 22$). Thus the investor's one-year rate of return from this hypothetical stock is 15 percent.

$$\text{RoR} = \left[\frac{1 + (22 - 20)}{20}\right] \times 100$$

$$\text{RoR} = 15$$

The total rate of return of 15 percent can be decomposed into a 5 percent dividend return, based on the purchase price, and a 10 percent appreciation in share price.

$$\text{RoR} = [1/20 \times 100] + [2/20 \times 100]$$

$$15 = 5 + 10$$

To introduce possible capital changes into the example, assume that near the end of the year the stock is split 2 for 1, and that the new shares are priced at $11 at year-end. Then the investor holds two shares valued at $11 each so that, adjusted for the stock split, the terminal value per original share is $22 (i.e., $11 × 2 shares).

Portfolio returns are calculated on a basis similar to that for individual stocks. To illustrate, assume an investor places $1000 in each of three separate stocks. The price of the first stock (S_1) is $20, of the second stock (S_2) is $10, and of the third stock (S_3) is $50. Investing $1000 in each of the three stocks, the investor's initial portfolio value is $3000; and he holds 50 shares of S_1, 100 shares of S_2, and 20 shares of S_3. As presented in Table 2-2, the investor is then assumed to receive some cash dividends during the year and to hold the same portfolio at the end of the year.

The one-year rate of return on the portfolio of three stocks can be com-

Table 2-2. Annual Rate-of-Return Calculation from a Hypothetical Three-Stock Portfolio

Stock (a)	Initial Investment (b)	Asked Price per Share at Beginning of Year (c)	Number of Shares Held (b) ÷ (c) (d)	Dividends per Share Received during Year (e)	Total Dividends Received during Year (d) × (e) (f)	Bid Price per Share at End of Year (g)	Terminal Portfolio Value (h)	Rate of Return (i)
S₁	$1000	$20	50	$1	$50	$22	$1100	+15%
S₂	1000	10	100	0	0	13	1300	+30
S₃	1000	50	20	2	40	48	960	0
Total........			170		$90		$3360	

$$\text{Rate of Return} = \frac{90 + (3360 - 3000)}{3000} \times 100$$

$$\text{RoR} = \frac{90 + 360}{3000} \times 100$$

$$\text{RoR} = 15$$

puted in the same way as the one-year rate of return for one stock. The formulation is as follows:

$$RoR = \left[\frac{D + (V_2 - V_1)}{V_1}\right] \times 100$$

Where:

RoR = Rate of return, expressed as a percentage.
D = Total cash dividends received during the year.
V_2 = End-of-year value of the total portfolio.
V_1 = Beginning of year value of the total portfolio.

The figures above are appropriately adjusted for stock splits and cash-equivalent distributions (such as rights with a market value).

Thus, based on the total dollar values presented in Table 2-2, the one-year rate of return on the total portfolio is 15 percent, of which 3 percent can be visualized as the dividend return and 12 percent as the increased value of the portfolio.

The total portfolio return of 15 percent is the same as the arithmetic mean of the individual rates of return of the different stocks in the portfolio. From Table 2-2, the individual returns are 15 percent, 30 percent, and 0 percent, so that the mean of this set of three numbers is as follows:

$$15\% = \frac{15\% + 30\% + 0\%}{3}$$

The calculated portfolio return of 15 percent is the same as the arithmetic mean of the individual stock returns because the investor is assumed to place an equal amount ($1000) into each of the three securities.

Four Principal Assumptions

The assumed investor strategy in this study is one of acquiring equal dollar amounts of each security at the start of each holding period. This procedure is neutral in that *each security receives equal initial weight* in the portfolio.

Dividends and other cash receipts are assumed not to be reinvested. Instead, such *cash receipts are assumed to be withdrawn* by the investor.

Purchases are made at the asked price quoted at the start of the year, while the subsequent valuation of the portfolio is at the bid price quoted at the end of the holding period. As explained in Chapter 1 (pages 8–

21

9), this procedure provides explicit recognition of *transaction costs* incurred in buying and selling securities in OTC markets.

Finally, no income tax assumptions are built into the rate-of-return calculations; not because income taxes are unimportant, but because of the wide range of possible income tax assumptions. These would reflect the investor's tax status (ranging from a tax-exempt institution to an individual with large amounts of earned income) and changes over time in the incomes of tax-paying investors. Given the many income tax possibilities, *rates of return are calculated exclusive of taxes*, an assumption that provides consistency across the study. Individual investors will want to consider such pre-tax calculations in relation to their individual tax rates.

Rate of Return from Portfolios of National OTC Stocks: An Illustration

Figure 2-2 portrays the one-year rate of return from a representative portfolio of national OTC stocks in 1969. The rate of return from this portfolio of thirty stocks is −29.7 percent. This return figure rests on the previously specified rate-of-return framework and the assumptions concerning (1) equal weights, (2) dividend withdrawal, (3) transaction costs, and (4) pre-tax calculations.

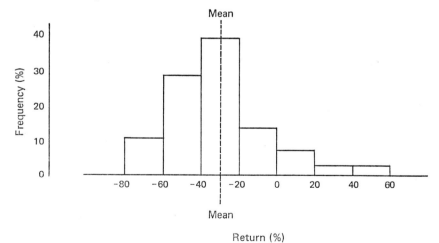

Figure 2-2. Distribution of returns from a random sample of thirty national OTC stocks, 1969. (Source: Text.)

Indexes versus Rates of Return

Note, however, that in addition to portraying the total portfolio return of −29.7 percent, Figure 2-2 provides a distribution of the rates of return for the various stocks in the portfolio. To illustrate, three of the thirty stocks had rates of return falling in the class interval of −60 to −80 percent; at the other extreme, two of the thirty stocks had one-year rates of return falling in the class intervals of 20 to 60 percent. As previously demonstrated, the assumption of equal weights results in the total portfolio return of −29.7 percent, which is also the arithmetic average of the distribution of the individual rates of return on the thirty stocks. Although the arithmetic average is a widely used summary measure, investors can neglect useful information if they focus on averages without considering the distribution of component elements that make up the average.

During 1969 the NQB OTC Industrial Index declined by 0.8 percent.[8] This contrasts with the decline of about 30 percent calculated for the representative portfolio of national OTC stocks.[9] How can such a difference in the measurement of the average performance of nationally traded OTC stocks be explained?

Twenty-one percentage points of the twenty-nine point difference is attributable to stock selection. As demonstrated earlier, the thirty-five stocks in the NQB Index differ significantly from stocks representative of the entire national OTC market. If the portfolio rate of return based on this study's assumptions is calculated for the thirty-five stocks in the NQB Index as of December 31, 1968, the one-year return for 1969 is −8.9 percent. Figure 2-3 presents the distribution of rates of return on the component thirty-five securities. The distribution is bimodal, with one group of stocks returning between 20 and 40 percent and another group returning between zero and −20 percent. Also, one of the stocks had a negative rate of return between −60 and −80 percent. Thus a distribution of individual rates of return provides more information than just a summary average figure.

Much of the remaining difference, between −0.8 and −8.9 percent, reflects the weighting of the thirty-five stocks in the NQB portfolio. The figure −8.9 percent is based on each of the thirty-five component stocks

8. As announced by OTC Market Information Bureau and reported in *Over-the-Counter Securities Review*, January 1970, p. 3.

9. This illustration compares two samples of the national OTC market — the NQB Index of thirty-five stocks and a random sample of thirty stocks. The analyses in subsequent chapters are based on *distributions* of random portfolios, so that the focus then is on the mean and other parameters of sampling distributions.

Returns in OTC Stock Markets

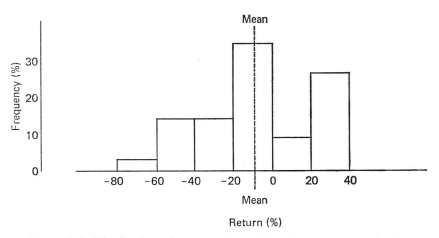

Figure 2-3. Distribution of returns from thirty-five stocks constituting the NQB Index of OTC industrial stocks, 1969. (Source: Stocks as of year-end 1968 identified in *O-T-C Market Chronicle*, January 2, 1969, p. 17; for computation, see text.)

having equal weight; for example, an investor is assumed to place $1000 in each of the stocks at the beginning of 1969. In contrast, the figure −0.8 percent is computed on a "Dow Jones basis," which means that the higher priced stocks are weighted more heavily in the portfolio. Such unequal weighting results in a return different from that based on an assumption of equal weights. Examination of the rates of return of the thirty-five stocks indicates that the ten stocks with the highest returns have an average initial share price of $72, which is more than twice the average share price of $31 for the ten stocks with the lowest returns. The heavier weighting of the relatively successful high-priced shares pulls up the total portfolio return over what it would be if it were based on an assumption of equal weight for each stock in the sample. Notably, this analysis applies only to the year 1969, and it is only intended to demonstrate the impact of alternative weighting assumptions.

Intermarket Comparisons of Rates of Return

The assumptions and implied investor strategy used in this study were selected for three reasons. One, they represent important features of the investment process, for example, transactions costs. Two, they are neutral, i.e., there is equal initial investment in each security. Three, they are simi-

24

lar to those used in studies of NYSE-listed stocks conducted by members of the Center for Research in Securities Prices at the University of Chicago, under the supervision of Professors Lawrence Fisher and James H. Lorie. These studies were initiated in response to the practical question, What has been the experience of investors in NYSE-listed stocks? [10] The Fisher and Lorie studies provide important measures of investor experience in NYSE stocks. They are based on highly reliable data, and the rate-of-return calculations are available in published form for time periods between 1926 and 1965.

Although not completely coterminus, the period examined in this OTC study overlaps that of the NYSE studies, thus facilitating intermarket rate-of-return analyses. Such comparisons offer, for the first time, information about the spectrum of stock markets described in Chapter 1.

10. Lawrence Fisher and James H. Lorie, "Rates of Return on Investments in Common Stocks," *Journal of Business*, January 1964, vol. 37, pp. 1–21.

3 Returns from the National Over-the-Counter Market

SHORT-RUN AND LONG-RUN RETURNS from national OTC portfolios are presented and analyzed in this chapter. In addition, these returns are compared with those available from NYSE portfolios. All statistical tests in this and subsequent chapters are at the 95 percent confidence level.

Rates of Return: One-Year Holding Periods

Table 3-1 shows mean one-year returns from national OTC portfolios for each year from 1946 through 1969. Chapter 1 explained that, for this study, samples of thirty securities were randomly drawn from the population of national OTC stocks at the beginning of each year. For each sampled stock, market information, such as prices, dividends, and capital changes, was then obtained for the subsequent five years. When subsequent information for five years is obtained, the set of sampled stocks for *any one year* is expanded to a maximum of 150 observations.[1] From each year's

1. To illustrate, for 1950 there are data on the thirty stocks drawn for that year plus data on the stocks drawn in the preceding four years, 1946–49. Although some of the sample stocks from preceding years left the national OTC market by year-end 1949, principally to go to registered stock exchanges, 115 of the 120 remained in the 1950 population of national OTC stocks. For each of the years 1950–69, there are between 119 and 145 sample stocks from which to construct representative portfolios.

Returns from the National OTC Market

set of up to 145 sample OTC stocks, 100 portfolios of thirty stocks each are randomly drawn. Each year's mean return from 100 portfolios is presented in Table 3-1.[2]

Table 3-1. One-Year Returns from National OTC Portfolios, 1946–69[a]

Year	Mean Portfolio Return (%)	Year	Mean Portfolio Return (%)
1946	−20.0	1958	43.3
1947	−12.0	1959	8.1
1948	−13.9	1960	−0.8
1949	2.5	1961	30.3
1950	28.1	1962	−18.7
1951	4.7	1963	2.2
1952	5.1	1964	11.2
1953	−1.4	1965	30.7
1954	24.5	1966	−9.0
1955	7.3	1967	82.4
1956	−2.8	1968	36.5
1957	−18.1	1969	−29.9

[a] Based on 100 randomly generated thirty-stock portfolios in each year.

The mean of the series of twenty-four one-year national OTC returns is 7.9 percent. This measure is relevant for investors who typically hold their investments for short periods, in this case, one year. This average is not the return earned on holding one portfolio from 1946 through 1969; rather it is the average of all the one-year returns, each of which is based on the assumption that the investor purchases a new portfolio of thirty national OTC stocks at the beginning of each year.

Figure 3-1 is a frequency distribution of the set of one-year national OTC returns during the entire time span 1946–69. In fourteen of the twenty-four years the returns are positive, while in the other ten years the returns are negative. For these twenty-four one-year returns the arithmetic average (7.9) is higher than the median of 3.6 percent, indicating that occasional very high returns "pull up" the arithmetic average.

How does the preceding average national OTC return compare with that of one-year returns from NYSE portfolios? The Fisher and Lorie studies of returns from NYSE stocks during the time period 1926–65 permit comparisons for the subperiod 1946–65, when measures of one-year portfolio returns in both markets are available. During this twenty-year

2. Each mean portfolio return from this simulation process also can be estimated from the sample mean of the component stocks. The simulation process is used because it generates distributions of portfolio returns.

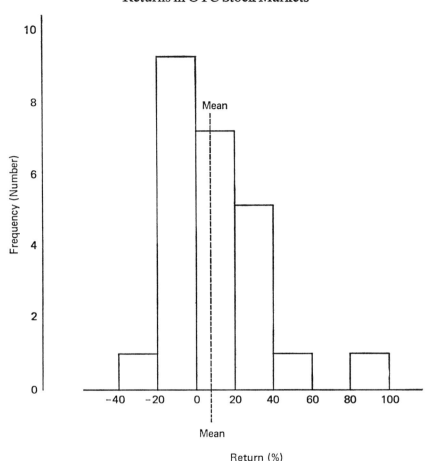

Returns in OTC Stock Markets

Figure 3-1. Distribution of one-year returns from national OTC
portfolios, 1946–69. (Source: Table 3-1.)

period, portfolios made up of thirty-two NYSE stocks provide positive returns in thirteen years.[3] This is similar to the national OTC returns, which
are positive in twelve of the years. However, focusing on the average of
the twenty one-year returns shows that the mean NYSE return is 13.8

3. The NYSE returns are based on data for portfolios of thirty-two stocks shown
in Lawrence Fisher and James H. Lorie, "Some Studies of Variability of Returns on
Investments in Common Stocks," *Journal of Business*, April 1970, vol. 43, Table A-1.
These portfolios have two more stocks than the portfolios used in this study. Exam-
ination of the Fisher and Lorie data suggests that this is not an important difference.
The data presented there have been converted into a rate-of-return format.

percent. In contrast, during the same time period (1946–65), the mean national OTC return is 5.5 percent.[4] Thus, during these twenty years, the one-year NYSE returns are 8.3 percentage points higher, on average, than the national OTC returns.

Also, the one-year returns from the two markets can be compared over time. In only one of the twenty years (1946–65) does one market show a positive return when the other shows a negative return. In the other nineteen years the mean returns from the two markets have the same sign. Thus the one-year rates of return in the two markets are positively correlated ($r = +0.92$).

Superior returns are more *frequent* from NYSE portfolios than they are from national OTC portfolios. In sixteen of the twenty years, NYSE returns are greater. If returns in the two markets are, on average, equal over time, then one would expect national OTC returns to be higher in ten of the years, with NYSE returns being higher in the other ten years. However, the actual ratio of superior returns, sixteen to four in favor of NYSE portfolios, is significantly different from the hypothesized equal split.[5]

It is also important to analyze the *magnitude* of the differences in returns. By what amount, on average, do NYSE returns exceed national OTC returns? Figure 3-2 portrays the annual differences between mean portfolio returns in the two markets.[6] In sixteen years mean NYSE returns exceed national OTC returns by, on average, 10.84 percentage points. Conversely in the four years when the national OTC returns exceed those from NYSE portfolios, the average superiority is 2.0 percentage points. The practical implications of these relationships are striking. The average amount of superior returns from national OTC portfolios is insufficient to offset their relative infrequency. Mathematically the preceding relation-

4. This twenty-year average of 5.5 percent is less than the figure of 7.9 percent calculated over the longer time period 1946–69. The latter figure is higher because of the relatively high one-year returns in 1967–68.

5. Binomial test.

6. For each of the twenty years, 1946–65, the difference is calculated between the average portfolio return from national OTC stocks and the average portfolio return from NYSE stocks. It is this set of twenty differences that is presented in Figure 3-2. The average of the distribution of differences (8.3 percent) is the same as the previously calculated difference between the mean returns of the distributions of one-year returns from NYSE portfolios (13.8 percent) and national OTC portfolios (5.5 percent).

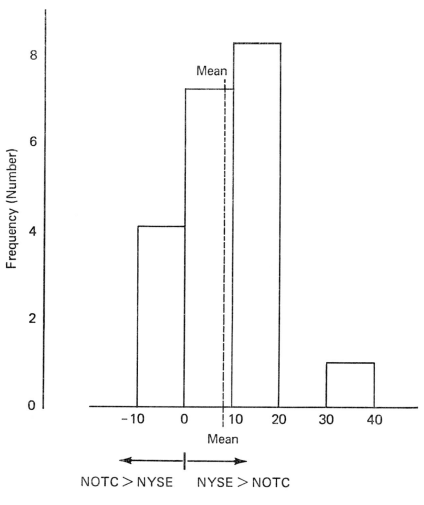

Figure 3-2. Distribution of differences between one-year returns from national OTC and NYSE portfolios, 1946–65. (Source: National OTC data derived from Table 3-1. NYSE data derived from Fisher and Lorie, "Some Studies of Variability of Returns on Investments in Common Stocks," *Journal of Business*, April 1970, Table A-1.)

ships of the average superiority of NYSE portfolios can be formulated as follows:

$$\text{Mean difference} = \frac{16(10.84) - 4(2.00)}{20} = 8.27$$

This indicates that during the twenty years under consideration the average superiority of NYSE portfolios is 8.3 percent, as portrayed by the mean of the distribution of differences (Figure 3-2).

Analyses of Longer Holding Periods

Important differences in average return relationships emerge as representative national OTC portfolios are held for longer time periods. The preceding section examined only one-year returns; this section extends the analysis to holding periods of three and five years. Such focus on one-, three-, and five-year holding-period returns serves as a convenient procedure for approximating shorter and longer run portfolio returns.

For holding periods of various lengths, Figure 3-3 illustrates distributions of returns from the portfolios of thirty national OTC stocks, randomly drawn at the beginning of each year from 1946 through 1969.[7] Thus, portfolio composition is held constant, so that returns on the same initial portfolios can be examined for one, three, and five years. Also, by focusing only on the different random portfolio of each of twenty-four years, there is little likelihood of overlap among the data over time.

The top segment of Figure 3-3 portrays the distribution of the series of one-year national OTC returns during 1946–69. The mean of this distribution is 5.3 percent. But note the dispersion around this central value. For four of the twenty-four years, the one-year return is between −20 to −30 percent; and in one year the return is between +60 to +70 percent. Furthermore, ten of the twenty-four one-year returns are negative.

As holding-period length increases, however, the distributions of returns become less dispersed and fewer negative returns appear. Thus the three-year returns cluster more tightly around the mean value of 12.8 percent, and only three years show negative returns. The five-year returns cluster even more tightly around the mean value of 14.7 percent, and there are no negative values. Thus, as the length of holding period increases from one to five years, the mean return increases, the distribution of returns be-

7. For the one-year holding periods, this is a subset of the many randomly selected portfolios in each year on which the analysis in the preceding section is based.

Returns in OTC Stock Markets

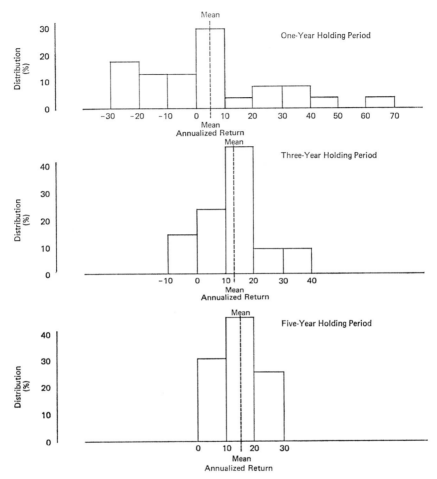

Figure 3-3. Distributions of annualized returns from representative national OTC portfolios for various length holding periods, 1946–69. (Source: Based on random samples of thirty stocks in each base period.)

comes tighter, and fewer negative values appear. For these distributions of one-, three-, and five-year returns portrayed in Figure 3-3, the coefficients of variation are 3.2, 0.8, and 0.4, confirming the observable increase in the tightness of the distributions.

The absence of negative returns when the portfolios are held for five years implies that their total cash flows and terminal values are at least

32

equal to the amount of the initial outlay. This absence of absolute loss is accompanied by a reduced opportunity for very high annualized returns. The highest such five-year return is in the category of +20 to +30 percent compared to the highest one-year return in the category +60 to +70 percent. Thus as the magnitude of extreme outcomes is reduced for the longer holding periods, there is an increased likelihood of obtaining returns close to the average.

Long-run returns from these national OTC portfolios also can be

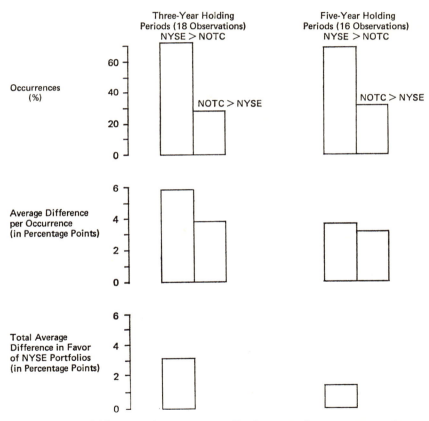

Figure 3-4. Differences between annualized returns from representative national OTC and NYSE portfolios for various length holding periods, 1946–65. (Source: National OTC data based on random samples of thirty stocks in each base period. NYSE data derived from Fisher and Lorie, "Some Studies of Variability of Returns on Investments in Common Stocks," *Journal of Business,* April 1970, Table A-1.)

compared to mean returns from NYSE portfolios.[8] As outlined in Figure 3-4, for three- and five-year holding periods the relative frequency of superior returns from NYSE portfolios is about 70 percent. For the five-year holding periods, this frequency is not significantly different from an hypothesized equal split.[9] The higher national OTC returns, when they exceed NYSE returns, are insufficient to compensate for their infrequency. This is shown in the lower sections of Figure 3-4. The average difference in favor of NYSE portfolios is 3.2 percent for three-year holding periods and 1.5 percent for five-year holding periods. This comparative analysis of holding periods of different lengths indicates that, on average, national OTC portfolios provide lower returns than do NYSE portfolios. However, this relationship is less adverse as holding-period length increases.

Impact of Transaction Costs

Practical measures of portfolio management cannot ignore transaction costs. Therefore the preceding analyses are based on returns which include transaction costs.[10]

To ignore transaction costs in measuring portfolio returns results in an overstatement of investor experience. To measure such overstatement, rates of return from the twenty-four representative OTC portfolios were recalculated on the assumption that the stocks *could be purchased* at their *bid* prices. If transaction costs, as measured by the price spread, are disregarded, the average one-year portfolio return for the total time span 1946–69 is found to be 14.5 percent, which contrasts with the figure 5.3 percent when estimated transaction costs are included.[11]

For the subperiod 1946–65, during which NYSE return measures are available, the mean one-year national OTC return is 14.0 percent, when

8. Fisher and Lorie "Some Studies of Variability of Returns on Investments in Common Stocks."

9. Binomial test.

10. In their various studies of rates of return from NYSE stocks, Fisher and Lorie recognize the need to include transaction costs. In their initial published study they state, "In this study actual New York Stock Exchange round-lot commission rates, as they existed on all purchase, sale, and re-investment dates, have been included in the calculations; . . ." "Rates of Return on Investments in Common Stocks." Thus, importantly, their rate-of-return measures can be compared with this study's calculations because both studies explicitly provide for transaction costs.

11. The impact of transaction costs is greater for one-year return measures than it is for longer period return measures. For longer holding periods the transaction cost is averaged over a greater number of years.

transactions costs are excluded. In the same time period, the mean one-year NYSE return is 13.8 percent. The similarity in average one-year portfolio returns is confirmed by the fact that in ten of the twenty years the NYSE returns were higher while, conversely, the national OTC returns were higher in nine of the twenty years. (In the one remaining year, the calculated returns were similar.)

Thus, even when national OTC returns are computed *without* transaction costs, and NYSE returns are computed *with* transaction costs, the national OTC portfolios do not show significantly higher returns. This analysis of the impact of transaction costs confirms a principal conclusion of this chapter, that national OTC portfolios do not provide higher returns, over time, than NYSE portfolios.

4 Returns from Regional Over-the-Counter Markets

THE PRINCIPAL QUESTION in this chapter is, Do portfolio returns from regional OTC stocks differ from those of nationally traded stocks? As has already been mentioned, the five regional OTC markets analyzed in this study are Atlanta, Chicago, Minneapolis-St. Paul, St. Louis, and San Francisco. Each of these geographically diverse cities is a regional financial center, as evidenced by its being the location of a Federal Reserve Bank. Also, in each city, a principal daily newspaper provides price quotations for regionally traded OTC stocks during the time span 1955–69, the only exception being St. Louis for which quotations are unavailable in the first part of 1955. Representative portfolios of thirty stocks are selected from every market at the beginning of each of the fifteen years. However, in years when less than thirty stocks are reported in a regional OTC market, all available stocks are included. A table summarizing the number of stocks in each portfolio, by year and by market, is presented as Appendix 2. All sample portfolios are based on random samples.

Returns from Aggregate Regional OTC Markets

To provide an overall view of regional OTC markets, the five markets are aggregated in this section of the chapter. Aggregation consists of combining stocks from each of the five markets into sets containing as many as 150 stocks in certain years. This procedure gives approximately equal weight to each market, and this provides a basis for assessing regional markets in general.[1] From these aggregated yearly sets of regional OTC stocks, 100 portfolios of thirty stocks each are drawn. (This procedure can result in the same stock being in more than one simulated portfolio.) The mean portfolio return for each year is presented in Table 4-1.

Table 4-1. One-Year Returns from Regional and National
OTC Portfolios, 1955–69[a]

Year	Aggregate Regional OTC Market Mean Portfolio Return (%)	National OTC Market Mean Portfolio Return (%)
1955	10.0	7.3
1956	−2.7	−2.8
1957	−20.4	−18.1
1958	36.5	43.3
1959	13.0	8.1
1960	−7.2	−0.8
1961	15.1	30.3
1962	−37.6	−18.7
1963	1.9	2.2
1964	4.8	11.2
1965	12.9	30.7
1966	−14.5	−9.0
1967	116.4	82.4
1968	45.6	36.5
1969	−28.8	−29.9

[a] Based on 100 randomly generated thirty-stock portfolios in each market in each year. (See text.)

To provide a basis for comparison, the one-year returns from national OTC portfolios, too, are given in Table 4-1. Examination of these two series of OTC annual returns shows that in nine of the fifteen years national OTC returns are higher than regional OTC returns. However, although relatively higher returns are *more frequent*, the split is not significantly different from that which can be explained by chance.[2] Also, the average of these one-year returns is 11.5 percent for national OTC

1. Disaggregated returns for each of the five regional OTC markets are portrayed in Figure 4-2.

2. Binomial test.

Returns in OTC Stock Markets

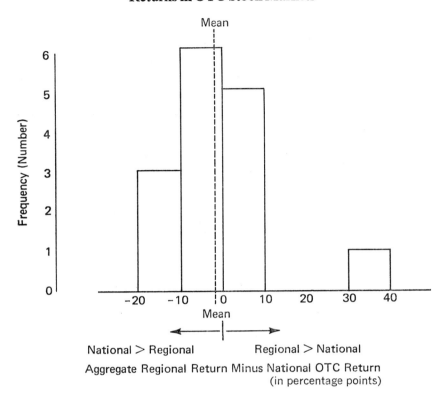

Figure 4-1. Distribution of differences between one-year returns from regional and national OTC portfolios, 1955–69. (Source: Table 4-1.)

portfolios compared to 9.7 percent for the regional portfolios, a difference that is not statistically significant.[3]

The differences in one-year returns between these two OTC markets are shown in Figure 4-1. The dashed line marks the average difference of 1.8 percentage points in favor of national OTC portfolios. In one year — 1967 — the mean regional return is more than 30 percentage points greater than the mean national OTC return. This difference is notable for its magnitude and infrequency. In summary, there are no strong differences between one-year returns from aggregate regional OTC portfolios and those from national OTC portfolios.

One-year returns from regional OTC portfolios also can be compared

3. T-test.

Returns from Regional OTC Markets

with returns from NYSE portfolios during the time period 1955–65.[4] The average regional OTC return is lower in each of these eleven years. If the distribution of differences in one-year returns is considered, it is seen that the mean difference is 12.0 percentage points in favor of NYSE portfolios. Although based on only eleven years, this analysis indicates that regional OTC portfolios provide significantly lower one-year returns, on average, than do NYSE portfolios.[5]

Returns in Five Regional OTC Markets

Not only can the regional OTC markets be analyzed on an aggregated basis, but the five markets also can be examined individually to determine whether there are major differences among such markets. Figure 4-2 portrays, on a year-by-year basis (1955–69), the portfolio returns in each of the five regional OTC markets. Notable in the figure are the high positive returns for 1967 and the large proportion of negative returns (about 40 percent) over the whole time period. In most years the five markets move together. The correlation coefficients of each market with every other regional OTC market are all positive and significant. In addition, the returns from the five regional OTC markets are positively correlated with the mean returns from national OTC portfolios.[6]

Annual portfolio returns in each of the five regional OTC markets can be directly compared to those of national OTC portfolios. To illustrate, the portfolio return from Atlanta OTC stocks in 1955 is 1.0 percent. In the same year, the mean return from national OTC portfolios is 7.3 percent. The difference between these two returns is 6.3 percentage points in favor of the national OTC portfolios. For the entire fifteen-year period 1955–69, the mean of this distribution of differences is −8.3 percentage points. This result is presented in Table 4-2, together with the average differences similarly calculated for each regional OTC market in comparison with the national OTC portfolios. Portfolio returns from Minne-

4. The Fisher and Lorie studies of NYSE returns currently provide portfolio returns only through 1965. "Some Studies of Variability of Returns on Investments in Common Stocks."

5. T-test. The period of comparison with NYSE stocks does not include recent years when regional portfolios show relatively large returns, for example 1967–68. However, as indicated in the comparison of returns in national versus regional OTC markets, the regional OTC markets are notable for infrequent very high returns.

6. Tests of correlation coefficients for the years 1956–69, when data for all OTC markets are available.

apolis-St. Paul stocks have a mean that is larger, but a median that is smaller than those of national OTC portfolios. This disparity reflects the 1967 Minneapolis-St. Paul return that is 160.4 percentage points greater than the comparative national OTC return.

For each year 1956–69, the portfolio return from each regional market can be arrayed from highest to lowest.[7] Thus, the markets with the highest returns are ranked with low numbers such as 1 and 2. If there is no significant differences among the market ranking over the time span, each mar-

7. The year 1955 is excluded from these ranking procedures because St. Louis OTC returns are not available.

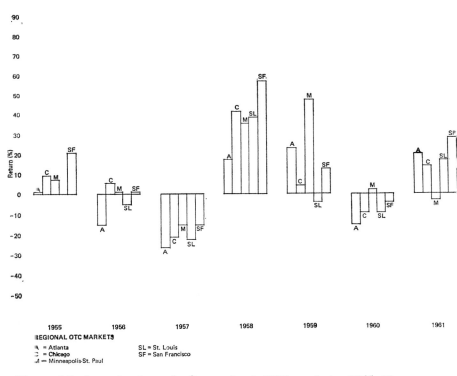

Figure 4-2. Annual returns in five regional OTC markets, 1955–69. (Source: Based on random samples in each market, each year. See text.)

Returns from Regional OTC Markets

ket will have 42 ranking points.[8] Table 4-3 presents the actual total ranking points for each market. The San Francisco and Chicago markets rank
higher than would be expected if the ranking points were equally distributed among the markets. However, the differences between actual and expected rankings are not statistically significant.[9]

8. For each year the total ranking values are 15 (i.e., $1 + 2 + 3 + 4 + 5$), and
there are fourteen years in the analysis. Therefore, the total of the ranking values
for the total time span is 210 (i.e., 15×14). The expectation is that, on average,
each of the five markets will have 42 ranking points ($210 \div 5$).

9. Friedman 2-way analysis of variance test.

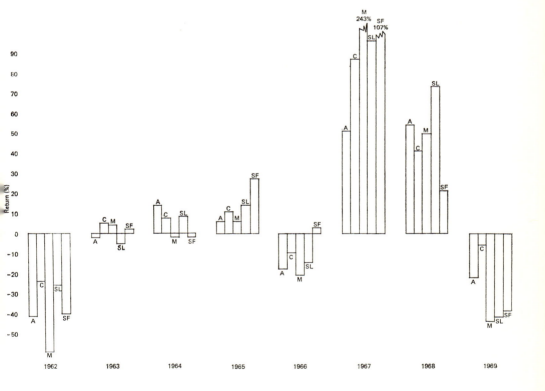

Table 4-2. Differences between One-Year Returns from
Regional and National OTC Portfolios, 1955–69[a]

Regional OTC Market	Differences in Percentage Points	
	Mean	Median
Atlanta	−8.3	−7.8
Chicago	−1.4	−3.1
Minneapolis-St. Paul	5.3	−0.3
St. Louis[b]	−3.4	−6.0
San Francisco	0.3	−0.5

[a] Regional returns are for randomly generated, thirty-stock
portfolios (one per market) each year; national returns are
means of 100 randomly generated portfolios each year.
[b] 1956–69. (See text.)

Table 4-3. Comparative Rankings of Regional OTC Markets
Based on Annual Portfolio Returns, 1956–69[a]

Regional OTC Market	Actual Number of Ranking Points
Atlanta	50
Chicago	37
Minneapolis-St. Paul	44
St. Louis	44
San Francisco	35

[a] The ranking procedure is based on an intermarket comparison. The market with the highest returns has the lowest
number (San Francisco). If there were no difference in relative market rankings over the total time span, each market
would have forty-two ranking points. (See text.)

Returns from Regional OTC Markets

Summary

Regional OTC returns are not significantly different from national OTC returns. This is based on comparisons of annual returns from aggregate regional OTC portfolios with returns from national OTC portfolios, 1955–69. This conclusion is further supported by disaggregating the regional OTC markets and examining annual returns in each of the five markets.

Annual returns from regional OTC portfolios are substantially less than NYSE returns, although for longer run holding periods this relative disadvantage of OTC returns is reduced.[10] Therefore, a principal conclusion is that portfolio returns from OTC stocks — both regional and national — are no greater than those available from NYSE portfolios.

10. This conclusion on longer run returns is based on a comprehensive analysis of the Minneapolis-St. Paul OTC market from 1946–67. See Roger B. Upson and Paul F. Jessup, "Risk-Return Relationships in Regional Securities Markets," *Journal of Financial and Quantitative Analysis,* January 1970, vol. 4, pp. 677–695; and Paul F. Jessup and Roger B. Upson, "Opportunities in Regional Markets," *Financial Analysts Journal,* March–April 1970, vol. 26, pp. 75–79.

PART III. Winners, Losers, and Diversification

5 High and Low Portfolio Returns

THREE PRINCIPAL QUESTIONS are discussed and answered in this chapter:

1. Do high portfolio returns differ significantly among OTC markets?

2. Are distributions of stock returns within high-return OTC portfolios significantly skewed, implying that high portfolio returns are associated with inclusion — by skill or chance — of some stocks that provide substantially above average returns that "pull up" the total portfolio return?

3. As a counterpoint, what are the attributes of low-return portfolios?

Previous chapters focus on average returns from 100 portfolios each year. In this chapter, "low" and "high" portfolio returns are defined as those at the first and ninth decile positions as shown by lines LL and HH in Figure 5-1.[1]

High Returns: A Multimarket Comparison

High-return national OTC portfolios provide positive returns in eleven of the fifteen years, 1955–69, and the distribution of these high returns is portrayed in the top segment of Figure 5-2. A similar distribution of high-

1. The first (low) and ninth (high) decile positions divide a distribution into the lowest 10 percent, middle 80 percent, and highest 10 percent. They are used as indicators of portfolios which show substantially below average and above average returns. They are not as extreme as minimum and maximum portfolio returns.

47

retur■ regional OTC portfolios is shown in the middle section of Figure 5-2. The means of these two distributions are 20.8 and 21.6 percent. Thus, on av∋rage *if* an investor holds the high-return portfolio each year in either OTC market, his average annual return is very similar. A distribution of the a■nual differences between high-return portfolios in the two markets is shcwn in the bottom section of Figure 5-2. The mean difference is not signifcantly different from zero.[2]

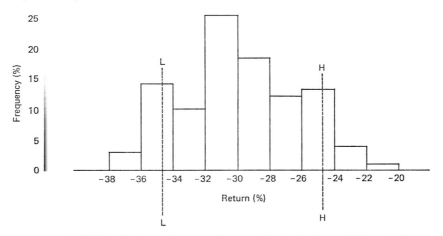

Figıre 5-1. Distribution of returns from national OTC portfolios, 1969. ⟨Source: Based on 100 randomly generated thirty-stock portfolios.)

Hi£h returns from OTC portfolios also can be compared with those from NYSE portfolios.[3] The time span 1955–65 was chosen because it is the lo gest period over which data on both OTC markets and the NYSE are available. For high-return portfolios, regional returns average 5.1 percentage points less than national returns, which in turn average 4.7 percentage points less than NYSE returns.[4] If high portfolio return is an investm∋nt goal, this analysis indicates that OTC portfolios are unlikely to provice higher returns than NYSE portfolios.

2. T-test.

3. F sher and Lorie, "Some Studies of Variability of Returns on Investments in Comm■n Stocks."

4. T]e frequency of high-return national OTC portfolios does not differ significantly from those of the two other markets. However, the frequency of high returns from r∈gional OTC portfolios and NYSE portfolios is significantly different (binomial test).

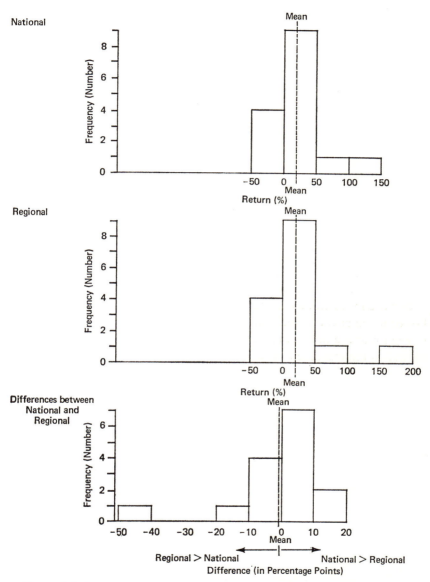

Figure 5-2. One-year returns from high-return OTC portfolios, 1955–69. (High-return portfolios are defined as those at the ninth decile in each year's distribution of 100 randomly generated portfolios.)

49

Skewness within Highest-Return OTC Portfolios

Are high returns typically achieved by holding portfolios of many relatively high-return stocks or by holding portfolios in which only several of the stocks provide exceptionally high returns? For example, assume that in a particular year high-return portfolios provide returns of 50 percent. Do such returns typically arise because the portfolios comprise thirty stocks, each of which returns about 50 percent, or because many of the stocks return less than 50 percent but several exceptionally successful stocks provide returns of between 100 to 300 percent, thus pulling up the portfolio return? These alternative possibilities are diagrammed in Figure 5-3.

Individual stock returns of Portfolio A cluster around the portfolio return of 50 percent while the individual stock returns of Portfolio B are more widely dispersed with the portfolio return of 50 percent being achieved by a combination of many lower returns and a few exceptionally high returns. As portrayed in Figure 5-3 the distribution of stock returns in Portfolio A is symmetrical while that of Portfolio B is positively skewed.

For each year from 1955 through 1969, the ten highest-return portfolios of national OTC stocks are tested for skewness. These ten portfolios of each year are those *at and above* the top decile position. In total, 150 portfolios are examined (ten each year times fifteen years). The results

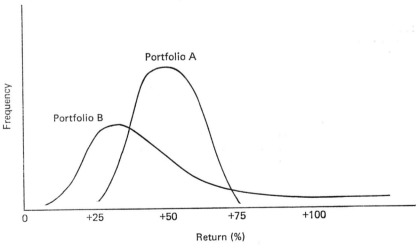

Figure 5-3. Distributions of stock returns
in two portfolios: An illustration

High and Low Portfolio Returns

are shown in Table 5-1. If symmetrical distributions and skewed distributions are equally likely, then the expectation would be seventy-five in each category. One hundred twenty-six of the national OTC portfolios are skewed, and all but two are positively skewed. This prevalence of skewness is improbable from a population of distributions equally split between symmetrical and skewed.[5] Similar testing of the highest-return regional OTC portfolios provides comparable results.

Prevalence of skewness in highest-return OTC portfolios indicates that such portfolios typically include several exceptionally successful (*ex post*) stocks in the portfolios.[6] If security analysts can identify such stocks *ex ante*, they can then provide important information for portfolio managers.

Table 5-1. Skewness of Distributions of One-Year Returns within Highest-Return OTC Portfolios, 1955–69[a]

Test Result	Number of Portfolios	
	National	Regional
Significantly skewed	126	131
Not significantly skewed	24	19
Total	150	150

[a] For definition of "highest-return portfolios," see text.

Low Returns: The Counterpoint

Low-return portfolios also can be compared across markets. Such an analysis of relatively poor portfolio performance provides a comparative measure of "downside risk" among markets.

Figure 5-4 presents frequency distributions of returns from the low-return national and regional OTC portfolios. As can be seen, the shapes and the means of the two distributions are not substantially different.

A distribution of yearly differences between the two OTC markets is shown in the bottom section of Figure 5-4. For low-return portfolios, in eleven of the fifteen years national returns exceed regional returns, and the average difference is 4.0 percentage points. Statistically the magnitude of low portfolio returns is not dissimilar in the two OTC markets.[7]

5. Chi-square test.

6. Arditti indicates that investors act as though they prefer positively skewed portfolios. Fred D. Arditti, "Risk and the Required Return on Equity," *Journal of Finance*, March 1967, vol. 22, pp. 19–36.

7. T-test.

51

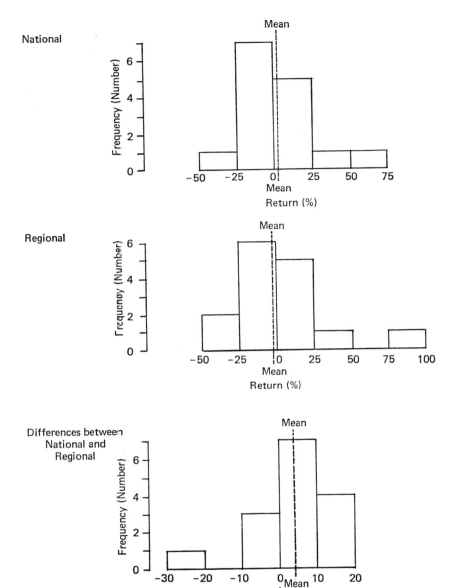

Figure 5-4. One-year returns from low-return OTC portfolios, 1955–69. (Low-return portfolios are defined as those at the first decile in each year's distribution of 100 randomly generated portfolios.)

52

High and Low Portfolio Returns

In the subperiod 1955–65, for low-return portfolios NYSE returns average 8.3 percentage points higher than national OTC returns.[8] Furthermore, these NYSE returns are 15.1 percentage points higher than those from low-return regional portfolios. Thus the downside risk is greater in OTC markets than on the NYSE.[9] These results indicate that investors seeking to avoid large one-year portfolio losses are more likely to achieve their objective by constructing NYSE portfolios.

Lowest-return portfolios are those *at and below* the first decile. For the period 1955–69, all 300 lowest-return national and regional OTC portfolios are tested for skewness. The results of this test are summarized in Table 5-2. Skewed and nonskewed distributions occur with almost equal frequency. When skewed, the distributions are generally positive. However, twelve of the lowest-return national OTC portfolios and nineteen from the regional OTC market exhibit significant negative skewness.

Table 5-2. Skewness of Distributions of One-Year Returns within Lowest-Return OTC Portfolios, 1955–69[a]

Test Result	Number of Portfolios	
	National	Regional
Significantly skewed	66	64
Not significantly skewed	84	86
Total	150	150

[a] For definition of "lowest-return portfolios," see text.

For both OTC markets, lowest-return portfolios generally do not demonstrate the positive skewness prevalent among highest-return portfolios. Nor do lowest-return portfolios typically have several stocks showing substantial losses that contribute to negative skewness. This implies that to avoid lowest-return portfolios, managers cannot rely on screening out small numbers of different stocks that may provide exceptionally adverse returns; rather they must try to avoid the many stocks that can contribute to low portfolio returns.

8. NYSE data derived from Fisher and Lorie, "Some Studies of Variability of Returns on Investments in Common Stocks."

9. In all years, 1955–65, the low-return NYSE portfolios have higher returns. This is significantly different, based on a binomial test.

6 High- and Low-Return Stocks

PORTFOLIO RETUENS from OTC markets are analyzed in preceding chapters. Because stock selection provides necessary inputs for portfolio managers, this chapter will examine returns from selected stocks.

The definitions of "high return" and "low return" used in this chapter are similar to those in the preceding chapter. A high-return stock is defined as the *one* located at the top decile of a distribution of one-year returns. Similarly, a low-return stock is the *one* located at the bottom decile of the distribution.

High-Return Stocks: Potential "Winners"

Are high-return stocks as likely to occur in OTC markets as in registered stock exchanges? Also, are returns from this category of stocks similar across markets? If the magnitudes are similar, security analysts trying to predict high-return stocks can focus their attention equally on stocks in various markets.[1] In contrast, if high-return opportunities are dissimilar across markets, security analysts should devote proportionately more resources to markets with greater potential.

1. However, even if high-return stocks are equally likely in various markets, an analyst may choose to focus on markets involving larger, more highly capitalized companies so that more clients can put more resources into such stocks.

High- and Low-Return Stocks

When high-return national OTC stocks are compared with high-return regional OTC stocks during the longest time period 1955–69, it is seen that neither the difference in frequency of occurrence nor magnitude of average difference is statistically significant.[2] Therefore, high returns are not significantly different in both OTC markets.

High-return OTC stocks also can be compared with those of the New York Stock Exchange. For high-return stocks, national OTC returns are less than NYSE returns in eight of the sixteen years (1950–65) for which comparative data are available.[3] The average difference is 0.4 percentage points. Thus high-return stocks are equally available in the national OTC market and in the NYSE.

A similar conclusion follows from comparing high returns of regional OTC and NYSE stocks. For the longest time span with comparative data (1955–65), high returns from regional OTC stocks are less than those from NYSE stocks in seven of eleven years and, on average, by 1.8 percentage points. Neither difference is statistically significant.[4]

Long-run holding-period returns from high-return OTC stocks can also be compared with those from NYSE stocks during four nonoverlapping periods of five years each from 1946 to 1965. In three of the four periods, NYSE stocks outperform national OTC stocks and average one percentage point more in annual return.[5] In summary, high-return stocks are not dissimilar among OTC markets and the NYSE. Thus, over many years, investors capable of selecting high-return stocks obtain similar returns from the various markets. As a counterpoint, low-return stocks will be analyzed later in this chapter.

Highest-Return Stocks

Extension of the previous analysis confirms that highest-return stocks are equally available in both the national and regional OTC markets. Highest-return stocks are defined as those *at and above* the ninth decile

2. The high return from national OTC stocks exceeds that from regional OTC stocks in nine out of fifteen years, but the national OTC returns average 7.5 percentage points less.

3. The frequency split of 8:8 also is not different from an hypothesized equal split.

4. Binomial test and T-test.

5. The limitation of the comparison to four time periods reflects the limited availability of data on NYSE stocks. See Fisher and Lorie, "Some Studies of Variability of Returns on Investments in Common Stocks."

of a distribution. For all OTC stocks included in this study between 1955 and 1969, the stock returns in the aggregate regional and national OTC markets are ranked, and the location (regional or national) of stocks in the top ten percent is identified.[6] In total there are 388 highest-return stocks. Of these, 190 are national and 198 are regional, not significantly different from the proportionate numbers of national and regional OTC stocks in the total data file for 1955–69.[7] Thus neither market provides a disproportionate number of highest-return stocks.

The relative occurrence of highest-return stocks also can be examined among the regional OTC markets. For each year 1956–69, every highest-return stock of the aggregate regional OTC market is classified according to its specific regional market.[8] If each market contributes an equal proportion of the highest-return stocks, then 10 percent of the sampled stocks in each of the five regional markets should be among the highest-return stocks of the aggregate category. However, the actual proportions from the five markets are as follows:

Regional Market	Percentage
Atlanta	8
Chicago	9
Minneapolis-St. Paul	13
St. Louis	8
San Francisco	12

This distribution is significantly different from the hypothesized equal-proportion distribution.[9] Proportionately more highest-return stocks are in the Minneapolis-St. Paul and San Francisco regional OTC markets, and proportionately fewer in the other three markets.[10]

6. To illustrate, the data file for 1955 has 139 one-year returns from national OTC stocks and 100 one-year returns from regional OTC stocks. These 239 returns are combined and arrayed and the twenty-four (10 percent) highest returns are identified as constituting thirteen national and eleven regional OTC stocks. Thus, the percentage of highest-return stocks in each market is about proportional to its percentage of the total 239 stocks.

7. Chi-square test.

8. The year 1955 is excluded from this analysis because of the unavailability of data concerning the regional OTC market in St. Louis.

9. Chi-square test.

10. The largest proportion of highest-return stocks is from the Minneapolis-St. Paul OTC market. However, before committing disproportionate resources to try to predict highest-return stocks in the Minneapolis-St. Paul markets, security analysts and investment managers should consider such factors as the typically small capital-

High- and Low-Return Stocks

Low-Return Stocks: Potential "Losers"

Analysis of low-return stocks indicates what can happen if investors fail to achieve average portfolio returns or to select high-return stocks. A low-return stock is defined as the *one* located at the lowest decile in a distribution of one-year stock returns. Are low stock returns similar across markets?

Low-return national OTC stocks have higher returns than similar regional stocks in thirteen of the fifteen years (1955–69) and the average difference is 10.9 percentage points in favor of national OTC stocks. The conclusion is that low returns from national OTC stocks are significantly higher than those from regional OTC stocks.[11] Thus substantial losses are less frequent for national than for regional OTC stocks.

Compared with low-return NYSE stocks, similar national OTC stocks provide lower returns in each of the sixteen years 1950–65, by an average of 15.5 percentage points. This outcome is unlikely to have occurred by chance. A similar two-way comparison of regional OTC and NYSE stocks shows the regional returns to be lower in each year 1955–65; the average difference is 25.6 percentage points. Thus low stock returns are significantly lower for both OTC markets than for the NYSE.[12]

Long-run holding-period returns also can be compared between low-return national OTC and NYSE stocks during four nonoverlapping periods of five years each from 1946 to 1965. The average return from low-return NYSE stocks is 5.4 percentage points greater than that from similar national OTC stocks. In addition, the NYSE returns are greater in three of the four periods.

In conclusion, low returns from OTC stocks are lower than those from NYSE stocks. In contrast high-return stocks are more evenly distributed among various markets. These conclusions indicate that while the probabilities of obtaining high-return stocks are not dissimilar across markets, probabilities of holding low-return stocks are greater in OTC markets.

Lowest-Return Stocks

Lowest-return stocks, defined as those *at or below* the bottom decile of a distribution, also can be compared across OTC markets. During 1955–69,

ization of firms with shares trading in this market (Chapter 9) and the average market return from such shares (Chapter 4).

11. T-test.

12. Binomial and T-tests are used in this section.

33 percent are from the national OTC market and 67 percent from regional OTC markets. This differs significantly from the 49:51 proportion of total individual stock returns in the two markets.[13]

Does the proportion of lowest-return stocks differ significantly among regional markets? The actual proportion of all lowest-return stocks contributed by each market (1956–69) is as follows:

Regional Market	Percentage
Atlanta	11
Chicago	3
Minneapolis-St. Paul	22
St. Louis	6
San Francisco	8

This distribution differs significantly from one in which the proportions are equal.[14] The Minneapolis-St. Paul market has the largest proportion of lowest-return regional OTC stocks. As previously shown, this market also has the largest proportion of highest-return stocks.

Summary

Selecting individual stocks in OTC markets is unlikely to offer higher returns over time than those available from NYSE stocks. In contrast, lower stock returns are concentrated in regional and national OTC markets. With this new insight into the parameters of returns from individual stocks, portfolio managers will want to consider carefully proffered opportunities in selected OTC stocks. They should not expect a disproportionate number of "winning" stocks to emerge from their selections in OTC markets, but rather they should be prepared for the potential of some large "losers."

13. Chi-square test.
14. Chi-square test.

7 Diversification

PORTFOLIO MANAGERS generally diversify among stocks in order to reduce the impact of adverse individual stock returns on a total portfolio return.[1] By what is basically an averaging process, the portfolio return lies somewhere between the extreme outcomes of the individual stocks.

Holding many common stocks can only reduce the risk of diverse returns from individual stocks. It cannot eliminate the "market risk" (or "systematic risk").[2] To illustrate, a widely diversified portfolio of NYSE stocks will have a return of about -10 percent if all NYSE stocks average a return of -10 percent in a particular year. In a declining stock market, a widely diversified portfolio will also decline. This "market risk" can be distinguished conceptually from the risk of individual stocks ("unsystematic risk"). Only unsystematic risk can be reduced through diversification among many stocks.

Since market risk cannot be removed from a portfolio of common

1. Most institutional investors are required to diversify their portfolios among various stocks. For example, the Investment Company Act of 1940 requires that mutual funds have no more than 5 percent of their total assets in any one stock. Thus required by law to hold at least twenty different stocks, many mutual funds, for various reasons, hold more than twenty different stocks.

2. "Market risk" means the risk inherent in the market, regardless of diversification. This title was applied by William F. Sharpe, "Capital Asset Prices: A Theory of Market Equilibrium under Conditions of Risk," *Journal of Finance*, September 1964, vol. 19, p. 439.

stocks, a principal purpose of diversification is to reduce unsystematic risk. Although diversification can be obtained by deliberately seeking stocks of companies with different industrial and economic characteristics, it is achievable also by increasing the number of different stocks in a portfolio. Each stock added is likely to have a different standard deviation of returns over time. Its fluctuations in rate of return are less than perfectly correlated with those of the stocks already in the portfolio. Consequently, the addition of stocks reduces portfolio risk, and the impact can be examined by measuring the relationship between the number of stocks in a portfolio and the standard deviation of the portfolio returns over time.

Figure 7-1 shows this diversification relationship for the national and regional OTC markets in the period 1960–69. As the number of stocks in a portfolio increases from one to fifty, the risk measure declines, with most of the reduction having occurred by the time the size of the portfolio has reached fifteen to twenty stocks.[3] The lowest value for the risk measure is obtained when a portfolio comprising all available stocks is analyzed; this value for each market is indicated by the horizontal lines in Figure 9-5. Thus these horizontal lines show the amount of market ("systematic") risk. Market risk is higher in the aggregated regional OTC market than in the national OTC market.

Alternative time periods produce varying estimates of the number of different stocks needed to reduce unsystematic risk. Analysis of the six overlapping five-year subperiods between 1960 and 1969 shows that the levels of market risk are unstable. In some periods market risk is almost twice that of other time periods. In all cases, however, the level of market risk is greater in the aggregated regional OTC market than in the national OTC market.[4]

3. The risk measure used in this analysis is the mean of twenty portfolio standard deviations. Thus for each size portfolio (one through fifty equally weighted stocks), twenty separate portfolios are selected and the standard deviation of annual portfolio returns from 1960 to 1969 is computed for each of the twenty portfolios. It is the mean of these twenty portfolio standard deviations that is shown as the risk measure in Figure 7-1. This procedure is similar to that used by John L. Evans and Stephen H. Archer, "Diversification and the Reduction of Dispersion: An Empirical Analysis," *Journal of Finance*, December 1968, vol. 23, pp. 761–767, and by Per B. Mokkelbost, "Unsystematic Risk over Time," *Journal of Financial and Quantitative Analysis*, March 1971, vol. 6, pp. 785–796.

4. Note that by holding thirty stocks in various OTC markets, unsystematic risk is, on average, effectively removed. What remains is market risk (systematic risk). Thus thirty-stock random portfolios are sufficiently large for measuring average market returns, as done in previous chapters.

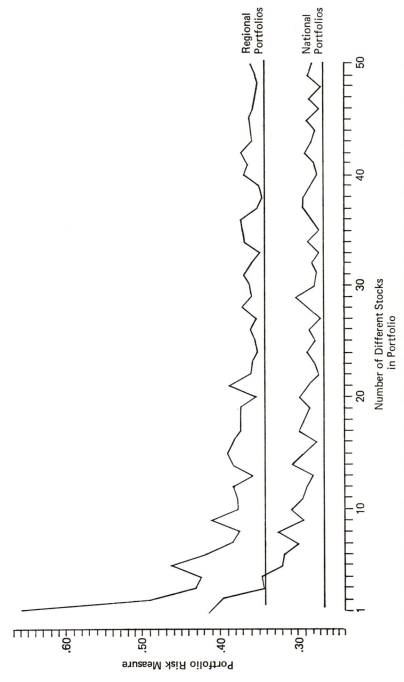

Figure 7-1. Diversification and reduction of dispersion in OTC markets, 1960–69. (Source: Chapter 7, note 3.)

61

Reduction of unsystematic risk by holding larger numbers of stocks has been analyzed by Evans and Archer, Fisher and Lorie, and Mokkelbost. Their analyses, however, have focused on NYSE stocks. Evans and Archer conclude that their results "raise doubts concerning the economic justification of increasing portfolio size beyond 10 or so securities, . . ." Fisher and Lorie also observe that "the opportunity to reduce dispersion by increasing the number of stocks in the portfolio is rapidly exhausted . . . Roughly, 40 percent of achievable reduction is obtained by holding two stocks; 80 percent, by holding eight stocks; 90 percent, by holding sixteen stocks; . . ." Mokkelbost also has examined the relationships between reduction of dispersion and numbers of stocks, concluding that the relationship is not stable over time.[5]

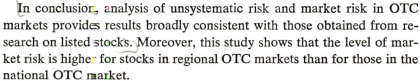

In conclusion, analysis of unsystematic risk and market risk in OTC markets provides results broadly consistent with those obtained from research on listed stocks. Moreover, this study shows that the level of market risk is higher for stocks in regional OTC markets than for those in the national OTC market.

5. Evans and Archer, "Diversification and the Reduction of Dispersion," p. 767. This analysis is based on 470 of the 500 stocks included in the Standard & Poor's 500 Stock Index, 1958–67. Fisher and Lorie, "Some Studies of Variability of Returns on Investments in Common Stocks," p. 117. Mokkelbost, "Unsystematic Risk over Time." This analysis is based on 699 of 900 stocks included in the Standard Statistics Compustat Tape for varying ten-year time periods 1952–67.

PART IV. Market Volatility

8 Relative Volatility: The Beta Controversy

PORTFOLIO THEORY recently has refined its concepts and measures of return. No longer are price indexes generally accepted as measures of portfolio performance over time. Now expected are inclusive rate-of-return measures that comprise both dividends and changes in capital values (Chapter 2).

Definition and measurement of "risk" similarly have received increasing attention from researchers and portfolio managers. Although there is not yet unanimity as to appropriate risk measures, recent research emphasizes relative volatility as a measurable risk concept.[1] Relative volatility focuses on the question, How volatile is a particular portfolio of stocks (or a single stock) relative to the general market? A portfolio that is more volatile than the general market can be classified as "riskier" than a second portfolio that is less volatile than the market. Numerical measures of the relative volatility of various portfolios thus provide quantitative measures of their relative "riskiness."

Beta Measures

An illustration of the measurement of relative volatility is provided in Figure 8-1. Basic inputs for the calculation are rates of return for successive time periods for a selected portfolio and for a "market portfolio."

---

1. For a recent review of the theory and practice of using Beta coefficients to measure "risk," see Chris Welles, "The Beta Revolution: Learning to Live with Risk," *Institutional Investor*, September 1971, vol. 5, pp. 21–27ff.

Such a market portfolio typically is represented by Standard & Poor's 500 Stock Index. The rate-of-return measures include dividends, price changes, and changes in capitalization (Chapter 2). In Figure 8-1, returns for the market portfolio are plotted on the horizontal axis, while rates of return from a selected portfolio are plotted on the vertical axis. The plot in the upper right-hand corner indicates that in the same time period the return of the selected portfolio was 20 percent while the market return was 17 percent.

The relative volatility of the portfolio is measured by the slope of the least-squares regression line of the portfolio returns on the market returns.

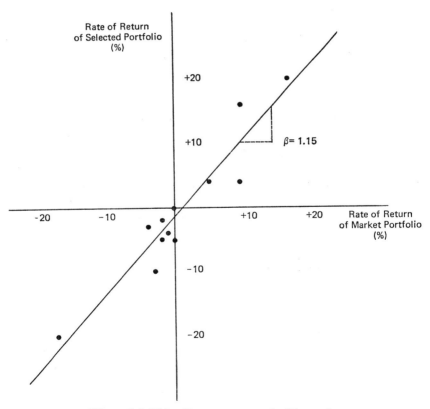

Figure 8-1. Using Beta measures: An illustration

Relative Volatility

This line is plotted in Figure 8-1. The slope of this line is also known as the Beta coefficient, and thus relative volatility is more popularly known as the "Beta" of the portfolio.

In Figure 8-1, the Beta for the selected portfolio is 1.15. This indicates that, on average, when the return on the market portfolio changes, the return on the selected portfolio changes by 1.15 times that amount. Thus returns from the selected portfolio are more volatile than those from the market portfolio. If Beta were exactly 1.0, then returns from the selected portfolio would be as volatile as those from the market portfolio; and if Beta were less than 1.0, then returns from the selected portfolio would be relatively less volatile. Betas for institutional portfolios typically range between 0.4 and 1.2.[2]

Betas of OTC Markets, 1955–69

Beta coefficients can be calculated for various portfolios of OTC stocks included in this study. In Figure 8-2 mean returns from portfolios of national OTC stocks for each year, 1955–69, are plotted against the rates of return of a market portfolio of NYSE stocks.[3] The regression line based on these fifteen rate-of-return observations is portrayed in Figure 8-2 by the solid line. This "line of best fit" is summarized by the following equation:

$$Y = -1.9 + 1.12X$$
$$R^2 = 0.55$$

The Beta coefficient is 1.12, indicating that over the time period 1955–69 the national OTC market was more volatile, on average, than the market portfolio of NYSE stocks.

Similarly in Figure 8-2 the annual returns from aggregate portfolios of regional OTC stocks are plotted relative to the NYSE market portfolio. A

2. Betas for portfolios such as those held by mutual funds, insurance companies, and bank trust funds have been computed in the last five years, and are frequently used as indicators of the risk level of a portfolio relative to a broadly diversified market portfolio. See the *Institutional Investor Study Report of the Securities and Exchange Commission* (Washington, D.C.: U.S. Government Printing Office, 1971), p. 333, Table IV-103.

3. For each of the years 1955–69, there are between 119 and 139 sample stocks in these representative national OTC portfolios. (Chapter 3, note 1.) Rates of return from the NYSE market portfolio are based on returns reported in Fisher and Lorie, "Some Studies of Variability of Returns on Investments in Common Stocks," for 1955–65 and computed on the Standard & Poor's 500 Stock Index for 1966–69.

regression line also is fitted to these fifteen observations, and its equation is as follows:

$$Y = -4.4 + 1.17X$$
$$R^2 = 0.37$$

The Beta coefficient shows that portfolios of regional OTC stocks were

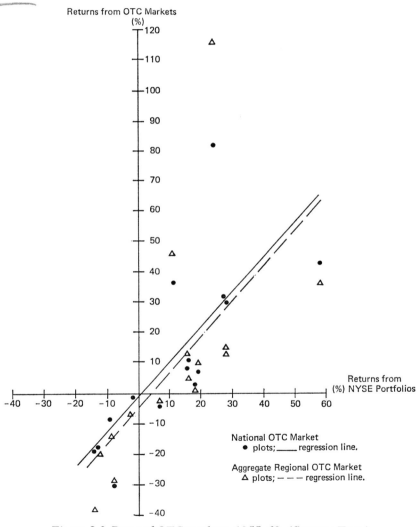

Figure 8-2. Betas of OTC markets, 1955–69. (Source: Text.)

more volatile than the market portfolio of NYSE stocks during 1955–69. It should be noted, however, that the R^2 of 0.37 indicates that much of the relationship between the regional market and the NYSE is "unexplained" by the regression equation.

In summary, the Beta coefficients for both national and regional OTC markets exceed 1.0, indicating that portfolio returns in these markets are, on average, more volatile than those from broadly diversified portfolios of NYSE stocks. Using relative volatility of returns as a risk measure, this implies that both principal components of the OTC market are "riskier" than those of the NYSE.

Instability of Beta

Are Betas stable over time? To answer this question the data underlying Figure 8-2 are calculated for five-year time spans, instead of the entire fifteen-year period. Betas for eleven overlapping five-year periods are given in Table 8-1.

Wide ranges for Beta are shown in Table 8-1. For the national OTC market, Betas for the five-year periods range from .83 to 2.11, which is narrower than the range for the aggregate regional market, .77 to 2.33. For both OTC markets, the range is large compared to the Beta computed for the total fifteen-year time span.

Furthermore, inspection of Table 8-1 suggests that the Beta measures in both markets have been shifting over time. In the earlier five-year pe-

Table 8-1. Betas of OTC Markets for Five-Year
Subperiods, 1955–69[a]

Time Period	National OTC Market	Aggregate Regional OTC Market
1955–59	.87	.79
1956–60	.83	.78
1957–61	.86	.77
1958–62	.86	.94
1959–63	.97	1.18
1960–64	.98	1.13
1961–65	1.14	1.25
1962–66	.97	1.03
1963–67	1.58	1.82
1964–68	1.63	1.83
1965–69	2.11	2.33

SOURCE: Text.

[a] Betas are calculated relative to NYSE returns.

riods the OTC markets are less volatile than the New York Stock Exchange. Only toward the end of the 1960s do the Beta measures indicate that the OTC markets are substantially more volatile than the New York Stock Exchange.

In summary, Beta measures for OTC market portfolios are unstable over time. This implies that statements about the relative volatility ("riskiness") of OTC markets should be qualified as to specific time periods. Furthermore, there is no strong evidence that relative volatility of OTC markets in the future can be directly predicted from past measures.

9 Market Attributes of Over-the-Counter Stocks

INVESTORS ARE CONCERNED with more than just returns and volatility of returns of their stock holdings. They also consider such attributes as dividend policies, total valuation of stocks traded in various markets, and movement of stocks among markets. New information about these market attributes is presented in this chapter.

Dividend Policies

Rate-of-return measures include both dividends and price changes. Do cash dividend policies differ among stocks in national and regional OTC markets? Furthermore, how do cash dividend policies of OTC stocks compare with those of NYSE stocks? The percentage of OTC stocks paying cash dividends declined during 1955–70, most noticeably after 1965 (Table 9-1). In contrast most NYSE stocks paid cash dividends in all those years. Because dividend-payment policies vary among markets and over time, comprehensive rate-of-return measures are more relevant than price indexes for measuring investment results. In addition, the smaller role of cash dividends is likely to make prices of OTC stocks more volatile, as investors emphasize probable patterns of future earnings.[1]

1. Burton G. Malkiel, "Equity Yields, Growth, and the Structure of Share Prices," *American Economic Review*, December 1963, vol. 53, pp. 1004–30.

Table 9-1. Percentage of Common Stocks Paying Cash Dividends in Preceding Year for Selected Years, 1955–70

Market	1955	1960	1965	1970
New York Stock Exchange ..	90	87	87	87
National OTC[a]	73	87	70	28
Regional OTC[a]	82	73	60	37

SOURCE: *New York Stock Exchange Fact Book*, 1971, p. 78.
[a] Based on random samples as of January 1.

Valuation

Distributions of quoted common stocks by total market value are shown in Figure 9-1. The distributions of market value calculations are based on representative samples of stocks from each OTC market as of the beginning of 1970.

Most national and regional OTC stocks are in the $1–10 million category.[2] Only regional stocks are in the smaller size categories below $1 million. The median value of national OTC stocks is similar to that of the Atlanta, Chicago, and San Francisco markets, but is significantly greater than that of the St. Louis and Minneapolis-St. Paul markets.[3]

A distribution of a random sample of NYSE stocks also is shown at the bottom of Figure 9-1. These stocks are in size categories greater than $10 million, which is consistent with one of the NYSE's listing criteria — that a publicly held common stock must have at least a total of $14 million in market value. Thus the median value of this sample of NYSE stocks is significantly greater than the median values of the stocks in the various OTC markets.[4]

Market values of OTC stocks during 1955–70 are summarized in Table 9-2. Regional OTC markets have twice as many stocks as the national OTC market in the category under $5 million. Conversely, regional OTC markets have only half as many stocks in the size categories of $10 million and above. These valuation attributes of OTC stocks also vary over time. (Appendixes 3–5.)

Price is an important component of valuation, and median bid prices

2. By contrast, in January 1970 the NQB Index underrepresents stocks having a market value of $1–10 million, and has no stocks with a market value less than $1 million (Chapter 2).

3. Median-comparison test.

4. Median-comparison test.

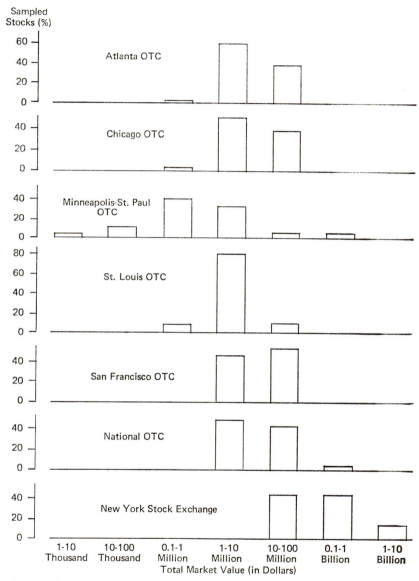

Figure 9-1. Distributions of samples of thirty common stocks, traded in various markets, by total market value of shares, January 1, 1970. (Source: Chapter 1.)

73

Returns in OTC Stock Markets

Table 9-2. Total Market Value of Individual Stocks in the
National and Regional OTC Markets: Aggregated
Data for Selected Years, 1955–70[a]

Total Market Value (in Millions of Dollars)	National OTC Market (%)	Regional OTC Markets (%)
Less than 5	25	50
5–10	22	22
10–15	5	10
15–20	7	4
20 and over	41	14
Total	100	100

SOURCE: Chapter 1.
[a] Based on random samples as of the beginning of 1955, 1960, 1965, and 1970.

Table 9-3. Median Bid Price for OTC Stocks for Selected
Years, 1955–70 (as of January 1)[a]

Market	1955	1960	1965	1970
National OTC	$12	$25	$13	$ 7
Regional OTC				
Atlanta	14	9	10	8
Chicago	21	18	10	11
Minneapolis-St. Paul	19	11	...[b]	2
St. Louis	NA[c]	13	8	8
San Francisco	19	28	12	14

SOURCE: Chapter 1.
[a] Based on random samples.
[b] Less than 50 cents.
[c] Not available.

for stocks in each OTC market are shown in Table 9-3. The Minneapolis-St. Paul market is characterized by low-priced stocks, especially in 1965 and 1970.

Movement among Markets

Over time some stocks leave OTC markets because they become listed on registered exchanges or merge with listed companies. The regular OTC quotation of some other OTC stocks ends for such reasons as cash sale, voluntary liquidation, or bankruptcy.

To quantify the transition process for national OTC stocks, random samples of thirty stocks are drawn at the beginning of 1955, 1960, and

Market Attributes of OTC Stocks

Table 9-4. Market Status after Five Years of Ninety National OTC Stocks[a]

Market Category	Number of Stocks	%
Listed on registered stock exchange	36	40
American 8		
New York 28		
Remained in national OTC market	34	38
Eastern OTC market[b]	7	8
Less publicized OTC quotation	7	8
Regular market quotation terminated	6	6
Total	90	100

[a] Derived from random samples of thirty stocks each in the years 1955, 1960, and 1965.

[b] This interim market category is described in Chapter 1.

1965. The five-year market histories of these stocks are summarized in Table 9-4.

The transition process for regional OTC stocks differs from that of national OTC stocks. The principal difference is that, over time, some regional stocks are reclassified from "regional" to "national" categories as they achieve broader investor interest. Table 9-5 outlines the transition process of common stocks in five regional OTC markets.

Table 9-5. Market Status after Five Years of Common Stocks in Five Regional OTC Markets[a]

Market Category	Number of Stocks	%
Listed on registered stock exchange	87	22
American 21		
New York 64		
Regional and Canadian 2		
National OTC market	102	25
Remained in regional OTC market	147	36
Less publicized OTC quotation	33	8
Regular market quotation terminated	22	5
Not available	18	4
Total	409	100

[a] Derived from random samples of thirty stocks each in the years 1955, 1960, 1965. At times a regional market had less than thirty stocks. In such cases, all available stocks were included. This explains the table's representing 409 stocks rather than the expected 450 (thirty stocks in each of five markets for three points in time). The criteria for defining these five markets, Atlanta, Chicago, Minneapolis-St. Paul, St. Louis, and San Francisco, are discussed in Chapter 1.

Nearly one-half of the randomly selected OTC stocks mature to broader markets within five years. Few go to regional stock exchanges as exclusive listings. Mergers into more widely held companies account for a substantial part of the maturing stocks. About one-third of the stocks remain in the same market category after five years. In summary, the population of OTC stocks is unstable over time.

Summary

Cash dividend policies and total market valuations of OTC stocks differ among OTC markets and vary over time. Furthermore, OTC stocks generally are in transition to broader markets or to comparative obscurity. Not only do OTC stocks thus vary among themselves, but they typically differ from NYSE stocks. These differences again demonstrate that research results based on NYSE stocks or narrow samples of national OTC stocks cannot be uncritically extended to OTC markets.

PART V. Conclusions

10 Opportunities in Over-the-Counter Markets

RETURNS FROM DIVERSE OTC markets are analyzed in this book, which focuses on the national OTC market and regional OTC markets in Atlanta, Chicago, Minneapolis-St. Paul, St. Louis, and San Francisco. These OTC analyses are compared with results of previously published, comprehensive studies of returns from stocks listed on the NYSE.

A framework integrating the nation's stock markets is presented in Chapter 1. Interrelationships among OTC markets and the registered stock exchanges are identified at a point in time. Also specified are the various transition paths by which many OTC stocks, over time, mature from regional OTC markets to the national OTC market and subsequently to the registered stock exchanges. Such an integrating framework of the nation's stock markets focuses attention on their diversity and interrelationships. Awareness of such diversity provides broader perspective to investors, public officials, and researchers who typically focus on specific markets, such as the New York Stock Exchange, without examining market interrelationships.

The only widely published measure of OTC market performance during 1946–69 is the OTC Industrial Index prepared by the National Quotation Bureau. However, as analyzed in Chapter 2, the component stocks in this index are not fully representative of the diverse population of OTC stocks. Furthermore, index numbers are dependent on their technical construction, such as weighting assumptions, and they provide only summary measures rather than distributions of outcomes.

In contrast to index numbers, rates of return provide more comprehensive measures of market performance (Chapter 2). The assumptions underlying this study's return measures are intended to reflect realistic investment strategies. Bias resulting from atypical case examples and posterior selection is avoided by analyzing representative portfolios constructed from OTC stocks actually available to investors at the beginning of each year.

Variability of Returns

Portfolio returns do not differ significantly among various OTC markets (Chapter 4). Although at times mean returns from some regional OTC markets exceed those from other regional markets and the national OTC market, over the total time span of this study average portfolio returns are not significantly higher or lower in any of the OTC markets.

Short-run portfolio returns from various OTC markets are significantly lower than those from NYSE stocks (chapters 3 and 4). An important factor in the computation of returns is transactions cost. Even if such transactions costs are disregarded for OTC portfolios and included for NYSE portfolios, the OTC portfolios do not provide significantly higher returns. For longer run holding periods, however, differences in returns are not statistically significant.

Market (systematic) risk is analyzed in national and regional OTC markets (Chapter 7). For portfolios of either national or regional OTC stocks, similar numbers of stocks are necessary to reduce unsystematic risk toward the level of each market's systematic risk. However, the level of systematic risk is higher for regional OTC markets than for the national OTC market.

Measurement of relative volatility, using Beta, shows OTC markets as more volatile than the New York Stock Exchange. However, the Beta measures are unstable over time.

Investors also can consider the cost of foregone opportunities. Returns from either high-return portfolios or high-return stocks are not substantially different in various markets. In contrast, there are significant differences between markets when low-return portfolios and low-return stocks are analyzed. Outcomes are significantly lower for regional OTC markets than for the national OTC market, which, in turn, are lower than for the New York Stock Exchange (chapters 5 and 6).[1]

Why Invest in OTC Stocks?

Over-the-counter markets, in comparison with the NYSE, are found to involve higher "risk" but not higher returns. In any holding period, a small proportion of OTC portfolios shows relatively advantageous risk-return relationships. Such occurrences are consistent with the findings of this study in which significant differences are based on a 95 percent confidence level. Why, then, do investors participate in OTC markets in which investment outcomes are dominated by those from the NYSE?

One, some investors who concentrate their portfolios in OTC stocks do not fully recognize the return parameters among stock markets. Their focus of attention and information is on successful stocks; stagnating and declining stocks are less publicized. This "information bias" is particularly important if such investors are, over time, a transient group initially attracted by case examples of successful OTC stocks. Over time they are exposed in practice to the more complete spectrum of OTC returns. These investors may then generally withdraw from OTC markets by totally withdrawing from the stock market, shifting to mutual funds and NYSE stocks, or focusing on OTC stocks similar to those listed on the NYSE. This process can be designated as the "transient OTC investor" hypothesis.

Two, other investors, over time, may be implicitly aware of intermarket relationships. Yet they continue to construct portfolios comprising only OTC stocks. Under these conditions, contemporary portfolio theory must reevaluate its underlying assumptions of rational behavior by investors. Such assumptions may not hold across various stock markets. Other variables to explain investor behavior must be introduced.[2]

1. While not explicitly analyzed in this study, the potential risks in OTC markets are also likely to be greater because, on average, OTC shares are those of smaller firms with greater "risk of ruin." Furthermore, in the absence of a specialist system the market for some OTC shares is less continuous over time. Empirical evidence for such additional risk dimensions in one regional OTC market is presented in Upson and Jessup, "Risk-Return Relationships in Regional Securities Markets."

2. For example, see Milton Friedman and L. J. Savage, "The Utility Analysis of Choices Involving Risk," *Journal of Political Economy*, August 1948, vol. 56, pp. 279–304.

Three, investors who do not have adequate knowledge of return parameters in various markets may include both listed and unlisted stocks in their portfolios. If the OTC stocks are not a dominant component of the total portfolio, these investors may seldom assess the relative contributions of the OTC stocks and the NYSE stocks in the context of their total portfolio performance.

Four, other portfolio managers may believe that returns from various markets are not perfectly correlated. Therefore, diversification across markets provides opportunities to reduce variance of total portfolio returns over time. Consistent with the diversification thesis, this study shows that OTC returns are less than perfectly correlated with NYSE returns. However, any reduction in variance is accompanied by a more than proportional reduction in combined return, because NYSE outcomes dominate OTC outcomes. Furthermore, investors can diversify among other assets not so dominated by NYSE returns.

In conclusion, if investor participation in OTC markets has been based on inadequate information about returns, then this book substantially reduces this information gap. Investors may expect future returns to be different, but now they can test their expectations against past results, as documented in this study.

Appendixes

Appendixes

One-Year Portfolio Returns in National and Regional OTC Markets, 1946–69[a]

Year	National OTC Market		Aggregate Regional OTC Market	
	Mean Port-folio Return (%)	Standard Devi-ation of Mean Portfolio Return (%)	Mean Port-folio Return (%)	Standard Devi-ation of Mean Portfolio Return (%)
1946	−20.0[b]	0.0[b]		
1947	−12.0[b]	4.3[b]		
1948	−13.9[b]	3.8[b]		
1949	2.5[b]	5.0[b]		
1950	28.1	14.5		
1951	4.7	4.7		
1952	5.1	5.0		
1953	−1.4	4.7		
1954	24.5	5.5		
1955	7.3	5.0	10.0	4.4
1956	−2.8	5.2	−2.7	4.0
1957	−18.1	4.7	−20.4	3.5
1958	43.3	8.6	36.5	7.8
1959	8.1	8.2	13.0	11.0
1960	−0.8	6.5	−7.2	7.0
1961	30.3	7.5	15.1	9.2
1962	−18.7	3.7	−37.6	5.0
1963	2.2	5.4	1.9	8.0
1964	11.2	5.3	4.8	8.2
1965	30.7	10.3	12.9	10.6
1966	−9.0	5.2	−14.5	6.0
1967	82.4	19.9	116.4	29.9
1968	36.5	8.1	45.6	17.2
1969	−29.9	3.7	−28.8	7.6

[a] Based on random samples. The aggregate regional OTC market is analyzed only for the subperiod 1955–69.

[b] The means and standard deviations for 1946–49 are based on portfolios drawn from less than 119 sampled stocks. See Chapter 3, note 1.

APPENDIX 2

Number of Stocks in Regional OTC Portfolios, 1955–69[a]

Year	Atlanta	Chicago	Minneapolis-St. Paul	St. Louis	San Francisco
1955	30	30	10	NA[b]	30
1956	30	30	20	12	30
1957	30	29	19	14	24
1958	30	30	18	16	29
1959	30	30	16	14	27
1960	30	30	30	26	27
1961	30	25	30	30	30
1962	30	30	30	30	30
1963	30	30	30	30	30
1964	30	30	30	30	18
1965	30	30	30	30	18
1966	27	30	30	28	27
1967	29	30	30	29	30
1968	23	30	30	21	30
1969	23	30	30	17	30

[a] Based on random samples of thirty stocks, if available. When less than thirty stocks are quoted in a regional OTC market, all are included. See chapters 1 and 4.

[b] Not available. See Chapter 1, p. 8.

APPENDIX 3

Total Value of Individual Stocks in Regional OTC Markets: Aggregated Data for Selected Years, 1955–70[a]

Total Market Value (in Millions of Dollars)	Atlanta	Chicago	Minneapolis-St. Paul	St. Louis[b]	San Francisco
Less than 5	56%	45%	66%	57%	25%
5–10	17	28	15	23	26
10–15	9	11	6	9	15
15–20	3	1	5	2	8
20 and above	15	15	7	9	25
Total	100	100	100	100	100

SOURCE: See Chapter 1.

[a] Based on random samples as of the beginning of 1955, 1960, 1965, and 1970.

[b] Excludes 1955 (not available).

NOTE: In appendixes 3–5, columns may not add to 100 because of rounding.

APPENDIX 4

Total Value of Individual Stocks in Regional OTC Markets:
Aggregated Data for Selected Years, 1955–70 (as of January 1)[a]

Total Market Value (in Millions of Dollars)	1955[b]	1960	1965	1970
Less than 5	45%	40%	63%	51%
5–10	25	22	22	20
10–15	11	13	6	10
15–20	6	4	1	4
20 and above	13	21	8	15
Total	100	100	100	100

SOURCE: See Chapter 1.
[a] Based on random samples.
[b] Excludes St. Louis in 1955 (not available).

APPENDIX 5

Total Value of Individual Stocks in the National OTC Market
for Selected Years, 1955–70 (as of January 1)[a]

Total Market Value (in Millions of Dollars)	1955	1960	1965	1970
Less than 5	47%	7%	27%	21%
5–10	20	10	27	31
10–15	3	10	0	7
15–20	3	3	7	14
20 and above	27	70	40	28
Total	100	100	100	100

SOURCE: See Chapter 1.
[a] Based on random samples.

APPENDIX 6

Company Names of National OTC Stocks
Analyzed in This Study, 1946–69

*(Names are rendered as they were in the year when the stock was
randomly selected)*

A L D, Inc.
Abbey Rents
Abitibi Power & Paper Co. Ltd.
Aerovox Corp.
Aetna-Standard Engineering Co. (Ohio)
Airline Foods Corp.
Alabama Mills, Inc.

Alico Land Development Co.
Amerex Holding Corp.
American Barge Line Co.
American Box Board Co.
American Building Maintenance
  Industries, Inc.
American Business Credit Corp.

Returns in OTC Stock Markets

American Commercial Barge Lines Co.
American District Telegraph Co. (N.J.)
American Financial Corp.
American Gas & Power Corp.
American Hardware Corp.
American Maize Products Co.
American Medical Enterprises, Inc.
American Phenolic Corp.
American Pipe & Construction Co.
American Wringer Co., Inc.
American-Saint Gobain Corp.
Anadite, Inc.
Anchor Coupling Co., Inc.
Angelica Uniform Co.
Anheuser-Busch, Inc.
Arden Farms Co.
Arizona Public Service Co.
Arkansas Valley Industries, Inc.
Arkansas Western Gas Co.
Arlan's Department Stores, Inc.
Armstrong Rubber Co.
Arrow-Hart, Inc.
Art Metal Construction Co. (Mass.)
Associated Spring Corp.
Atlanta Gas Light Co.
Automatic Retailers of America, Inc.
Automation Industries, Inc.
Avon Products, Inc.
Aztec Oil & Gas Co.

Bank Building & Equipment Corp.
 of America
Bareco Oil Co.
Bates Manufacturing Co. (Me.)
Belknap Hardware and Manufacturing
 Co.
Beneficial Corp.
Benguet Consolidated Mining Co.
Berkshire Fine Spinning Assoc., Inc.
Berkshire-Hathaway, Inc.
Beryllium Corp.
Billups Western Petroleum Co.
Bird & Son, Inc.
Black Hills Power & Light Co.
Blue Moon Foods, Inc.
Bohn Business Machines, Inc.
Botany Industries, Inc.
Bowser, Inc.
Brown & Sharpe Manufacturing Co.
Buckeye Steel Castings Co.
Buda Co.
Buffalo-Eclipse Corp.
Bullocks, Inc.
Burndy Corp.

Byllesby (H. M.) & Co., Inc.

Calbiochem, Inc.
California Oregon Power Co.
California Water Service Co.
Camden Forge Co.
Canadian Delhi Oil Ltd.
Canadian Superior Oil Co.
 of California Ltd.
Cannon Mills Co.
Capitol Records, Inc.
Caressa, Inc.
Carey (Philip) Manufacturing Co.
Carlisle Corp.
Carpenter Paper Co. (Omaha, Neb.)
Cascade National Gas Corp.
Ceco Steel Products Corp.
Central Electric & Gas Co.
Central Illinois Electric & Gas Co.
Central Louisiana Electric Co., Inc.
Central Maine Power Co.
Central Ohio Light & Power Co.
Central Telephone Co.
Central Vermont Public Service Corp.
Chance (A. B.) Co.
Charles of the Ritz, Inc.
Chicago Musical Instrument Co.
Cinecolor Corp.
Cinerama, Inc.
Citizens Utilities Co.
Cleveland Cliffs Iron Co. (Ohio)
Clow Corp.
Clyde Porcelain Steel Corp.
Coastal States Gas Producing Co.
Coca Cola Bottling Co. of New York,
 Inc.
Coleman Engineering Co.
Collins Radio Co.
Colorado Interstate Gas Co.
Colorado Milling & Elevator Co.
Columbia Baking Co.
Commerce Clearing House, Inc.
Commonwealth Gas Corp.
Commonwealth Telephone Co.
 (Dallas, Pa.)
Concord-Fabrics, Inc.
Connecticut Light & Power Co.
Consolidated Credit Corp.
Consolidated Freightways, Inc.
Consolidated Investment Trust
Consumers Power Co.
Continental Device Corp.
Continental Screw Co.
Continental Transportation Lines, Inc.

Appendix 6

Cowles Communications, Inc.
Crampton Manufacturing Co.
Crowell-Collier Publishing Co.
Cummins Engine Co.
Curtis Noll Corp.

DC International, Inc.
Dan River Mills, Inc.
Danly Machine Specialties, Inc.
Darling (L. A.) Co.
Dayton Corp.
Delhi-Taylor Oil Corp.
Delta Air Lines, Inc.
Derby Gas & Electric Corp. (Del.)
Detroit & Canada Tunnel Corp.
Detroit Harvester Co.
Diamond Crystal Salt Co.
Dickey (W. S.) Clay Manufacturing
    Co.
Dictaphone Corp.
Digitronics Corp.
Disney (Walt) Productions, Inc.
Documentation, Inc.
Doman Helicopters, Inc.
Donnelly (R. R.) & Sons Co.
Doyle Dane Bernbach, Inc.
Drackett Co.
Dravo Corp.
Du Mont (Allen B.) Laboratories, Inc.
Dun & Bradstreet, Inc.
Dunningcolor Corp.
Duriron Co., Inc.
Dwight Manufacturing Co.

Edgerton, Germeshausen & Grier, Inc.
El Paso Electric Co. (Tex.)
Electrolux Corp.
Elk Horn Coal Corp.
Emhart Manufacturing Co.
Erie Forge & Steel Corp.
Escon, Inc.
Ets-Hokin & Galvan, Inc.

Family Finance Corp.
Fanner Manufacturing Co.
Far West Financial Corp.
Federal Electric Products Co.
Federal National Mortgage Association
Federal Water & Gas Corp.
First Boston Corp.
First Surety Corp.
First Union Realty
Fisher Governor Co.
Florida Steel Corp.

Flying Tiger Line, Inc.
Foote Brothers Gear & Machine Corp.
Foremost Dairies, Inc.
Foster Grant Co., Inc. (Del.)
Foundation Co. (N.Y.)
Four Star Television Co.
Fownes Brothers & Co., Inc.
Fresnillo Co.
Friendly Ice Cream Corp.
Fritzi of California Manufacturing Co.

Garfinckel (Julius) & Co., Inc.
Gateway Chemicals, Inc.
General Aniline & Film Corp.
General Automotive Parts Corp.
General Crude Oil Co.
General Dry Batteries, Inc.
General Real Estate Shares
General Shale Products Corp.
General Waterworks Corp.
Genuine Parts Co.
Giant Portland Cement Co.
Giddings & Lewis Machine Tool Co.
Girltown, Inc.
Glass Fibers, Inc.
Glickman Corp.
Good Humor Corp.
Government Employees Financial Corp.
Grace (W. R.) & Co.
Greater Washington Investors, Inc.
Green (A. P.) Fire Brick Co. (Mo.)
Green Giant Co.
Green Mountain Power Corp.
Grey Advertising, Inc.
Grinnell Corp.
Gruen Watch Co.
Gulf Interstate Co.
Gulf Public Service Co., Inc.

Hagan Chemicals & Controls, Inc.
Hajoca Corp.
Hall-Scott Motors Co.
Haloid Xerox, Inc.
Hamilton Cosco, Inc.
Handy & Harman
Hanna (M. A.) Co.
Harris-Seybold Co.
Hartford Electric Light Co.
Haven Industries, Inc.
Helene Curtis Industries, Inc.
Heublein, Inc.
Higgins, Inc.
High Voltage Engineering Corp.
Hollingsworth & Whitney Co.

Hooker Electrochemical Co.
Hoover Co.
Housatonic Public Service Co.
Houston Corp.
Hoving Corp.
Howell Electric Motors Co.
Hudson Pulp & Paper Corp.
Hugoton Production Co.

Ideal Cement Co.
Indiana Gas & Water Co., Inc.
Infrared Industries, Inc.
Instrument Systems Corp.
Inter-County Telephone & Telegraph
  Co.
Intermark Investing, Inc.
International Bank (Washington, D.C.)
International Cellucotton Products Co.
International Furniture Co.
International Textbook Co. (Pa.)
Interstate Bakeries Corp.
Interstate Natural Gas Co., Inc.
Interstate Securities Co. (Del.)
Investors Diversified Services, Inc.
Iowa Beef Packers, Inc.
Iowa Electric Light & Power Co.
Iowa Public Service Co.
Iowa Southern Utilities Co.

Jack & Heintz, Inc.
Jamaica Water Supply Co.
Jervis Corp.
Jessop Steel Co.
Joslyn Manufacturing & Supply Co.

Kalamazoo Vegetable Parchment Co.
Kalvar Corp.
Kansas Gas & Electric Co.
Kansas-Nebraska Natural Gas Co., Inc.
Kearney & Trecker Corp.
Kellwood Co.
Kendall Refining Co.
Kerr-McGee Oil Industries, Inc.
Keta Gas & Oil Corp.
Keuffel & Esser Co.
Keyes Fibre Co.
Keystone Custodian Funds, Inc.
King Kullen Grocery Co.
Kold-Hold Manufacturing Co.

La Plante-Choate Manufacturing Co.
L'Aiglon Apparel, Inc.
Lake Arrowhead Development Co.
Landers, Frary & Clark

Lane Wood, Inc.
Lawyers Mortgage & Title Co.
Lear, Inc.
Liberty Aircraft Products Corp.
Liberty Fabrics of New York, Inc.
Liberty Loan Corp.
Littelfuse, Inc.
Loft Candy Corp.
Lone Star Steel Co.
Longchamps, Inc.
Long's Drug Stores, Inc.
Los Angeles Drug Co.
Ludlow Manufacturing & Sales Co.
Ludman Corp.
Luscombe Airplane Corp.
Lynch Communications Systems, Inc.

McBee Co.
MacFadden Publications, Inc.
McGraw (F. H.) & Co.
McLean Industries, Inc.
McLouth Steel Corp.
Macmillan Co., The
Madison Gas & Electric Co.
Maguire Industries, Inc.
Management Assistance, Inc.
Marmon-Herrington Co., Inc.
Mattel, Inc.
Medallion Pictures Corp.
Meister Brau, Inc.
Melpar, Inc.
Merchants Fast Motor Lines, Inc.
Merck & Co., Inc.
Mergenthaler Linotype Co.
Metal Goods Corp.
Mexican Eagle Oil Co., Ltd.
Mexican Gulf Sulphur Co.
Michaels Brothers, Inc.
Michigan Gas & Electric Co.
Michigan Gas Utilities Co.
Midas-International Corp.
Midwest Rubber Reclaiming Co.
Miles Shoes, Inc.
Miller Manufacturing Co.
Mississippi Shipping Co.
Mississippi Valley Gas Co.
Missouri Utilities Co.
Missouri-Kansas Pipe Line Co.
Modern Homes Construction Co.
Montrose Chemicals Co.
Moog Servocontrols, Inc.
Moore Drop Forging Co.
Moore-Handley Hardware Co.
Morris Plan Co.

Appendix 6

Mountain States Power Co.

Nalco Chemical Co.
Nathan Straus-Duparquet, Inc.
National Casket Co., Inc.
National Gas & Oil Corp.
National Paper & Type Co.
National Shirt Shops of Delaware, Inc.
National Tank Co.
National Transit Pump & Machine Co.
Naumkeag Steam Cotton Co.
New England Gas & Electric
  Association
New Jersey Natural Gas Co.
New Orleans Public Service, Inc.
Newmarket Manufacturing Co.
Newport Steel Corp.
Nicholson File Co.
Norris-Thermador Corp.
North America Coal Corp.
North European Oil Co.
Northwest Natural Gas Co.
Nu Enamel Corp.

Osgood Co.
Otter Tail Power Co. (Minn.)
Oxford Paper Co.
Oxy-Catalyst, Inc.
Ozite Corp.

Pacific Airmotive Corp.
Pacific American Investors, Inc.
Pacific Far East Line, Inc.
Pacific Power & Light Co.
Packaging Corp. of America
Pan American Sulphur Co.
Parker Appliance Co.
Pendleton Tool Industries, Inc.
Pepsi-Cola General Bottlers, Inc.
Permutit Co.
Peter Hand Brewery Co.
Petroleum Heat & Power Co.
Pfaudler Co.
Pioneer Natural Gas Co.
Placer Development Ltd.
Plymouth Cordage Co.
Plymouth Rubber Co., Inc.
Porter (H. K.) Co., Inc. (Pa.)
Portland General Electric Co.
Portsmouth Steel Corp.
Potash Co. of America
Preway, Inc.
Producers Cotton Oil Co.
Producing Properties, Inc.

Pubco Petroleum Corp.
Public Service Co. of Indiana, Inc.
Public Service Co. of New Hampshire
Public Service Co. of New Mexico
Punta Alegre Sugar Corp.
Purex Corp. Ltd.
Purolator Products, Inc.

Railweight, Inc.
Reeves Soundcraft Corp.
Remington Arms Co., Inc.
Remington Corp.
Republic Natural Gas Co.
Revere Racing Association, Inc.
Richardson Co.
Richmond Cedar Works
Ridge Tool Co.
Robertson (H. H.) Co.
Rockland Light & Power Co.
Rockwell Manufacturing Co.
Roddis Plywood Corp.
Rose Marie Reid
Royal Dutch Petroleum Co.
Royal Industries, Inc.
Russell Manufacturing Co.
Ryder System, Inc.

SSP Industries, Inc.
Safety Car Heating & Lighting Co.
St. Louis Shipbuilding-Federal Barge,
  Inc.
San Diego Gas & Electric Co.
San Jacinto Petroleum Corp.
Sawhill Tubular Products, Inc.
Scam Instrument Corp. (Chicago)
Schlitz (Jos.) Brewing Co.
Scientific Industries, Inc.
Scott & Fetzer Co.
Scovill Manufacturing Co.
Scranton Lace Co.
Scranton Spring Brook Water Service
  Co.
Seabrook Farms Co.
Sealed Power Corp.
Security Banknote Co. (Del.)
See's Candy Shops, Inc.
Seismograph Service Corp.
Selmer (H. & A.), Inc.
Seneca Falls Machine Co. (Mass.)
Shatterproof Glass Corp.
Shepard-Niles Crane & Hoist Corp.
Shulton, Inc.
Siegel (Henry I.) Co.
Signal Finance Corp.

91

Sioux City Gas & Electric Co.
Skiatron Electronics & Television Corp.
Skil Corp.
Small Business Investment Co.
  of New York, Inc.
Smith Industries International, Inc.
Smith, Kline & French Laboratories
Sonoco Products Co.
Soroban Engineering, Inc.
South Jersey Gas Co. (N.J.)
South Shore Oil & Development Co.
Southeastern Public Service Co.
Southern Advance Bag & Paper Co.
Southern California Water Co.
Southern Colorado Power Co.
Southern Natural Gas Co.
Southern Nevada Power Co.
Southern New England Telephone Co.
Southern Union Gas Co. (Del.)
Southwest Gas Producing Co., Inc.
Southwest Lumber Mills, Inc.
Southwest Natural Gas Co.
Southwestern Electric Service Co.
Southwestern Research & General
  Investment Co.
Southwestern States Telephone Co.
Speer Carbon Co.
Staco, Inc.
Staley (A. E.) Manufacturing Co.
Standard Milling Co. (Del.)
Standard Railway Equipment
  Manufacturing Co.
Stanley Works, The
Star Tank & Boat Co.
Stouffer Corp.
Strategic Materials Corp.
Strawbridge & Clothier
Stromberg-Carlson Co.
Struthers Wells Corp.
Stubnitz Greene Corp.
Suburban Propane Gas Co.
Superior Tool & Die Co.
Supervised Investors Services, Inc.
Susquehanna Corp.
Susquehanna Mills, Inc.

Tampax, Inc.
Tastee Freez Industries, Inc.
Tecumseh Products Co.
Telecoin Corp.
Telecomputing Corp.
Teledyne, Inc.
Telephone Utilities
Texas Eastern Transmission Corp.

Texas Gas Transmission Corp.
Texas Illinois Natural Gas Pipeline Co.
Texas Industries, Inc.
Texas National Petroleum Co.
Therm-O-Disc, Inc.
Tide Water Power Co.
Tidelands Oil Corp.
Tillie Lewis Foods, Inc.
Time, Inc.
Timely Clothes, Inc.
Title Guarantee & Trust Co. (N.Y.)
Toledo Scale Corp.
Towmotor Corp.
Tracerlab, Inc.
Trailmobile Co.
Trans-Texas Airways, Inc.
Transcontinental Gas Pipe Line Corp.
Transport Motor Express, Inc.
Trico Products Corp.
Tucson Gas & Electric Co.

Uarco, Inc.
Union Financial Corp.
United Artists Theatre Circuit, Inc.
U.S. Leasing Corp.
U.S. Sugar Corp. (Del.)
U.S. Truck Lines, Inc. of Delaware
United Transit Co. (Del.)
United Western Minerals Co.
Unitrode Corp.
Universal Match Corp.
Upson Co.
Utah Construction & Mining Co.
Utilities & Industries Corp.

Valley Gas Co.
Valley Mould & Iron Corp.
Vance, Sanders & Co., Inc.
Varian Associates
Victoreen Instrument Co.
Virginia Dare Stores Corp.

Wabash Magnetics, Inc.
Warner & Swasey Co.
Warwick Electronics, Inc.
Washington Steel Corp.
Watson Brothers Transportation
  Co., Inc.
Wayne Manufacturing Co.
Weissberg (H. R.) Corp.
Welch Grape Juice Co.
Wellman Engineering Co.
Werner Transportation Co.

West Penn Power Co.
West Point Manufacturing Co.
West Virginia Water Service Co.
Western Gold & Uranium, Inc.
Western Light & Telephone Co., Inc.
Western Natural Gas Co.
Western Publishing Co., Inc.
White Eagle Oil Co.
Whiting Corp.
Wiegand (Edwin L.) Co.
Wiley (John) & Sons, Inc.
Winslow Tele-Tronics, Inc.

Winters & Crampton Corp.
Wisconsin Power & Light Co.
Wometco Enterprises, Inc.
Wood Conversion Co.
Woodward Governor Co.
Wyle Laboraories

Yardney Electric Corp.
Yellow Transit Freight Lines, Inc.
Yolande Corp.
York Corrugating Co.
Yuba Consolidated Industries, Inc.

APPENDIX 7

Company Names of Regional OTC Stocks
Analyzed in This Study, by Market, 1955–69

*(Names are rendered as they were in the year when the stock was
randomly selected)*

ATLANTA

Abrams (A. R.), Inc.
Aerosonic Corp. (Fla.)
Air Control Products, Inc.
Airlift International, Inc.
Allen (R. C.) Business Machines, Inc.
Amarlite Corp.
American Art Metals Co.
Atlanta Motor Lodges, Inc.
Atlanta Paper Co.
Atlantic Co.
Atlantic Steel Co.
Atlas Finance Co., Inc.
Augusta Newspapers, Inc.
Automatic Merchandising, Inc.
Auto-Soler Co.

Bibb Manufacturing Co.
Billups Eastern Petroleum Co.
Brown Engineering Co.
Brunner Manufacturing Co.
Builtwell Homes, Inc.
Bush Hog, Inc.
Butler's, Inc.

Cagle's, Inc.
Carolina Freight Carriers Corp.
Cher-o-kee Photofinishers, Inc. (Tenn.)
Citizens & Southern Capital Corp.
Claussen Bakeries, Inc.

Clute Corp.
Coca Cola Bottling Co. of St. Louis
  (Del.)
Collyer Insulated Wire Co.
Continental Conveyor & Equipment Co.
Continental Gin Co.
Cousins Properties, Inc.
Crumpton Builders, Inc.

Denver Acceptance Corp. (Colo.)
Dixie Aluminum Corp.
Dynatronics, Inc.

Eckerd Drugs of Florida
Economy Auto Stores, Inc.

Farrington Manufacturing Co.
Fulton Investment Corp. (Atlanta, Ga.)

General Gas Corp.
General Minerals Corp. (Md.)
Genuine Parts Co.
Georgia Marble Co.
Georgia Shoe Manufacturing Co., Inc.
Glasrock Products, Inc.
Gordon Foods, Inc.
Gray Communications Systems, Inc.
Great Southern Real Estate Trust
Griggs Equipment, Inc.

Hav-a-Tampa Cigar Corp.
Haverty Furniture Companies, Inc.

Returns in OTC Stock Markets

Industrial Vinyls, Inc.
Inter-Mountain Telephone Co.

Jackson's Minit Markets, Inc. (Fla.)
Jebco, Inc.
Jewell (J. D.), Inc.
Johnny Reb, Inc.

Kellogg Co.

Leon Land & Cattle Co.
Liberty Loan Corp.

M & F Graphic Arts and Industrial
   Photographic Supply Co. (Ga.)
Marble Products Co. of Georgia
Minerals & Chemicals Corp. of
   America
Mississippi Shipping Co.
Mississippi Valley Gas Co.
Mobile Gas Service Corp.
Morton Manufacturing Corp.

National Data Corp.
National Food Products Corp.
National Pool Equipment Co.
North Carolina Telephone Co.

One-Hour Valet, Inc.
Oxford Chemical Corp.

Parker Petroleum Co., Inc.
Pecos Exploration Co.
Peter Hand Brewery Co.
Phoenix Investment Co.
Piedmont Aviation, Inc.
Piedmont Natural Gas Co., Inc.
Policy-Matic Corp. of America (Ga.)

Radiation, Inc.
Retail Credit Co.
Rice Broadcasting Co., Inc.
Rich's, Inc.
Rogers (John) Co.

Savannah Gas Co.
Savannah Sugar Refining Corp.
Scientific-Atlanta, Inc.
Scripto, Inc.
Seapak Corp.
Second Financial, Inc.
South Atlantic Gas Co.
South Georgia Natural Gas Co.
Southeastern Telephone Co.

Southern Airways, Inc.
Southern Bakeries Co.
Southern Cross Industries, Inc.
Southern Spring Bed Co.
Southern Syndicate, Inc.
Southland Investment Corp.
Space Craft, Inc.
Standard Container Co.
Sterling Discount Corp.
Super Stores, Inc.

TMT Trailer Ferry, Inc.
Tampa Marine Co.
Tekoil Corp.
Telechrome Manufacturing Corp.
Tennessee Natural Gas Lines, Inc.
Terminal Transport Co., Inc.
Thomaston Mills
Tradewinds Exploration, Inc.
Transcontinental Bus System, Inc.
Triumph Storecrafters Corp.
Tull (J. M.) Industries, Inc.

Uniservices, Inc.
United States Finance Co., Inc.

Walter (Jim) Corp.
Western Kentucky Gas Co.
Woodman Co., Inc.

CHICAGO

Acme Industries, Inc.
Allen (R. C.) Business Machines, Inc.
Allis (Louis) Co.
American Hair & Felt Co.
Ampco Metal, Inc.
Aqua-Chem, Inc.
Arcady Corp.
Armstrong Paint & Varnish Works, Inc.
Aurora Corp. of Illinois

Bankers Utilities Corp.
Barber-Greene Co.
Baxter Laboratories, Inc.
Beam (James B.) Distilling Co.
Bergstrom Paper Co.
Berns Air King Corp.
Birtcher Corp.
Birtman Electric Co.
Brown Fintube Co.
Bruning (Charles) Co., Inc.
Burgess Vibrocrafters, Inc.

Appendix 7

Calumet Industries, Inc.
Capitol Food Industries, Inc.
Carpenter Paper Co. (Omaha, Neb.)
Carson Pirie Scott & Co.
Caspers Tin Plate Co.
Central Fibre Products Co., Inc.
Central Steel & Wire Co.
Central Wisconsin Motor Transport Co.
Chamberlain Manufacturing Corp.
Chance (A. B.) Co.
Chicago, Aurora & Elgin Railway Co.
Chicago Aerial Industries, Inc.
Chicago Daily News, Inc.
Chicago Mill & Lumber Co.
Chicago Molded Products Corp.
Chicago Railway Equipment Co.
Classified Financial Corp.
Clayton Mark & Co.
Coleman Cable & Wire Co.
Combined Paper Mills, Inc.
Conn (C. G.) Ltd.
Consolidated Leasing Corp. of America
Consolidated Water Power & Paper Co.
Cook Electric Co.
Cornell Paperboard Products Co.
Cory Corp.
Crawford Corp.
Creamery Package Manufacturing Co.
Cribben & Sexton Co.
Curtis Companies, Inc.

De Jur-Amsco Corp.
Dean Milk Co.
Delta Electric Co.
Detroiter Mobile Homes, Inc.
Dowzer Electric, Inc.
Duncan Electric Co., Inc.

Fearn Foods, Inc.
Federal Sign & Signal Corp.
Foster-Forbes Glass Co.
Fred Harvey

G-R-I Corp.
Gateway Chemicals, Inc.
General Binding Corp.
Getz (William) Corp.
Gisholt Machine Co.
Glen Manufacturing Co.
Globe Steel Tubes Co.
Godfrey Co.
Grant Advertising International, Inc.
Gulf Coast Leaseholds, Inc.

Halo Lighting, Inc.
Handschy Chemical Co.
Hart-Carter Co.
Hawley Products Co.
Helene Curtis Industries, Inc.
Henry's Drive-In, Inc.
Hines (Edward) Lumber Co.
Hirsch (P. N.) & Co.
Hoerner Boxes, Inc.
Hubinger Co.
Hurletron, Inc.

Illinois Bell Telephone Co.
Illinois Tool Works, Inc.
Imperial-Eastman Corp.
Indiana Limestone Co., Inc.
Interstate Hosts, Inc.
Irwin (Richard D.), Inc.

Jacobsen Manufacturing Co.
Jefferson Electric Co.
Johnson Service Co.
Joslyn Manufacturing & Supply Co.

Kirsch Co.
Koehring Co.
Krueger (W. A.) Co.

Laclede Steel Co.
Lake Central Airlines, Inc.
Lakeside Industries, Inc.
Larsen Co.
LaSalle Street Capital Corp.
Lawter Chemicals, Inc.
Lincoln Telephone & Telegraph Co. (Del.)
Lindberg Steel Treating Co.
Luminator-Harrison, Inc.

MacWhyte Co.
Marley Co.
Marquette Corp.
Marsh Supermarkets, Inc.
Mastic Asphalt Corp.
Mayer (Oscar) & Co., Inc.
Mercantile Financial Corp.
Metal Goods Corp.
Meyer (Geo. J.) Manufacturing Co.
Meyercord Co.
Midas-International Corp.
Middle States Telephone Co. of Illinois
Minerals Engineering Co.
Modern Materials Corp.
Monarch Marking System Co.

Returns in OTC Stock Markets

Morris Paper Mills

National Aluminate Corp.
National Health Enterprises, Inc.
National Terminals Corp.
Nielsen (A. C.) Co.
North American Van Lines, Inc.
North Central Airlines, Inc.
Northern Plastics Corp.
Northwestern Steel & Wire Co.
Nuclear-Chicago Corp.
Nunn-Bush Shoe Co.

Obear-Nester Glass Co.
Oilgear Co.
Old Fort Industries, Inc.
Opelika Manufacturing Corp.
Ozite Corp.

Packard Instrument Co., Inc.
Pepsi-Cola General Bottlers, Inc.
Pettibone Mulliken Corp.
Pheoll Manufacturing Co., Inc.
Pickering Lumber Corp.
Poor & Co.
Portable Electric Tools, Inc.
Powers Regulator Co.
Preway, Inc.

R. C. Can Co.
RTE Corp.
Racine Hydraulics, Inc.
Rap Industries, Inc.
Ray-o-Vac Co.
Red Owl Stores, Inc.
Reynolds & Reynolds Co.
Roberts & Porter, Inc.
Roper Industries, Inc.
Rothmoor Corp.

St. Clair Manufacturing Corp.
Sales Follow-Up Corp.
Scholz Homes, Inc.
Schultz Sav-O Stores, Inc.
Schuster (Ed.) & Co., Inc.
Scott (O. M.) & Sons Co.
Scott Radio Laboratories, Inc.
Scruggs-Vandervoort-Barney, Inc.
Sealed Power Corp.
Servicemaster Industries, Inc.
Shelby Williams Industries, Inc.
Snap-on Tools Corp.
Stange Co.
Sun Electric Corp. (Del.)

Supercrete Ltd.

Tally Corp.
Tele-Tape Productions, Inc.
Thomas Industries, Inc.

Unicare Health Services, Inc.
U.S. Reduction Co.
Universal Telephone, Inc.

Vapor Corp.
Vendo Co.
Voi-Shan Industries, Inc.

Wagner Industries, Inc.
Walnut Grove Products Co., Inc.
Warren-Bradshaw Exploration Co.
Weco Products Co.
Wells-Gardner Electronics Corp.
Werner Transportation Co.
West Ohio Gas Co.
Wilding, Inc.
Woodward Governor Co.

Zeigler Coal & Coke Co.

MINNEAPOLIS-ST. PAUL

Aaro Rents
Alpha Distributing, Inc.
American Electronics Co.
American Hoist & Derrick Co.
American Micro Devices, Inc.
American Monarch Corp.
American Plan, Inc.
Apache Oil Corp.
Apache Realty Corp.
Applebaum's Food Markets, Inc.
Aqua-Lectric, Inc.

Bankers Agency, Inc.
Beck's, Inc.

Charter Design & Manufacturing Corp.
Chromo-O-Lite Co.
Commercial Chemical Co., Inc.
Commercial Resins Corp.
Consolidated Freightways, Inc.
Continental Marine Corp.
Control Data Corp.

Data Display, Inc.
Data Management, Inc.

Appendix 7

Data Products Corp.
Data Systems Devices of Boston, Inc.
Dexon, Inc.
Diginamics, Inc.
Donaldson Co., Inc.
Doughboy Industries, Inc.
Durox of Minnesota, Inc.

Eagle Wash Corp.
Economics Laboratory, Inc.
El Taco of Minnesota, Inc.
Electric Power Door Co., Inc.
Electro Nuclear Systems Corp.
Electro-Craft Corp.
Electro-Mation Co.
Electro-Sensors, Inc.
Empire Associates, Inc.
Environ Electronic Laboratories, Inc.
Equity Capital Co.
Erickson Corp.

Fiber Products, Inc.
Fiberite Corp.
Fire Engineers, Inc.
First Midwest Capital Corp.
Flame Industries, Inc.
Flo-Tronics, Inc.
Flour City Ornamental Iron Co.
Food Corp. of America
Forman, Ford & Co.

General Electronic Control, Inc.
General Magnetics, Inc.
General Tape Corp.
General Trading Co. (St. Paul, Minn.)
Glass Products, Inc.
Gopher Container Corp.
Green Giant Co.

Henry's System Northwest, Inc.

Imperial Financial Services, Inc.
Inland Marine Corp.
International Finance Corp.
International Housing Corp.
Interplastics Corp.
Investors Diversified Services, Inc.
Investors Syndicate of Canada Ltd.
Ivey Corp.

Jansen Electronics Manufacturing, Inc.
Johnson (E. F.) Co.
Johnson (J. N.) Co., Inc.
Josten's, Inc.

Kahler Corp.
Knutson Companies, Inc.
Kodiak, Inc.

Lakeside Industries, Inc.
Leyghton-Paige Corp.
Li'l General Stores, Inc. (Minn.)

McCloud River Lumber Co.
McQuay, Inc.
Magna-Tek, Inc.
Magnetic Controls Co.
Marketing Factors, Inc.
Marquette Corp.
Mars Industries, Inc.
Marshall-Wells Co.
Medical Investment Corp.
Medtronics, Inc.
Midtex, Inc.
Midwest Marine
Midwest Technical Development Corp.
Midwest Television Systems, Inc.
Minerals Technology Corp.
Minneapolis Associates, Inc.
Minneapolis Scientific Controls Corp.
Minnesota & Ohio Oil Corp.
Minnesota Capital Corp.
Minnesota Electronics Co.
Minnesota Natural Gas Co.
Minnesota Pharmaceutical
    Laboratories, Inc.
Minnesota Valley Natural Gas Co.
Miratel Electronics, Inc.
Modern Controls, Inc.
Motco, Inc.
Motor Travel Service, Inc.
Moulded Products, Inc.
Murphy Finance Co.

Naegele Advertising Companies, Inc.
National Connector Corp.
Norris Dispensers, Inc.
North American Royalties, Inc.
North Central Airlines, Inc.
Northwest Paper Co.
Northwest Plastics, Inc.
Northwest Systems Corp.
Northwestern States Portland Cement
    Co.
Nu-Line Industries, Inc.
Nucleonic Controls Corp.

Oakridge Holdings, Inc.
Otter Tail Power Co. (Minn.)

PHC, Inc.
Pacific Gamble Robinson Co.
Patterson (M. F.) Dental Supply Co.
of Delaware
Pawnee Corp.
Photo-Control Corp.
Pik-Quik, Inc.
Pioneer Investment Corp.
Plastics Corp. of America, Inc.
Printed Circuits, Inc.
Product Design & Engineering, Inc.
Programmed & Remote Systems Corp.
Publishers Vending Services, Inc.
Puratronics, Inc.
Pyroil Co.

Quarterback Sports Federation, Inc.

Rap Industries, Inc.
Rayette, Inc.
Red Owl Stores, Inc.
Regal Industries, Inc.
Research, Inc.
Reuter, Inc.
Rocket Research Corp.
Rosemount Engineering Co.

Safety Systems, Inc.
St. Paul Ammonia Products, Inc.
St. Paul Union Stock Yards Co.
Schaper Manufacturing Co., Inc.
Scherr-Tumico, Inc.
Schjeldahl (G. T.) Co.
Scientific Computers, Inc.
Shopco, Inc.
Silent Knight Security Systems, Inc.
Space Structures, Inc.
Spectacular Products, Inc.
Sterner Lighting, Inc.
Super Valu Stores, Inc.
Superior Electronics Co.
Swenko Research & Development, Inc.

T-K Products Co.
Tal-Cap, Inc.
Technalysis Corp.
Tedesco, Inc.
Telex Corp.
Texota Oil Co.
Theradyne Corp.
Theratron Corp.
Thermotech Industries, Inc.
Timesavers, Inc.
Toro Manufacturing Corp.

Transistor Electronics Corp.
Tri-State Displays, Inc.
Tronchemics Research, Inc.
Tru-Line Design & Engineering Co.

Unimed, Inc.
United Fabricators & Electronics, Inc.
United States Brass Corp.
Universal Discount Stores, Inc.

Van Dusen Air, Inc.

Waco-Porter Corp.
Washington Machine & Tool Works,
Inc.
Washington Scientific Industries, Inc.
Whitehall Electronics Corp.
Winter (Jack), Inc.
Wood Conversion Co.
World Toy House, Inc.
Writing Toys Corp.

York Enterprises, Inc.

ST. LOUIS

Adler Electronics, Inc.
Albee Homes, Inc.
Aloe (A. S.) Co.
Ambassador Oil Co.
American Auto Stores, Inc.
American Realty and Petroleum
Corp. (Okla.)
American Safety Equipment Corp.
American Self Service Stores, Inc.
American Snacks, Inc.
Angelica Uniform Co.
Arkansas Valley Industries, Inc.

Bank Building & Equipment Corp.
of America
Be-Mac Transport Co., Inc.
Biederman Furniture Co.
Broderick & Bascom Rope Co.

Carboline Co.
Century Acceptance Corp.
Chance (A. B.) Co.
Clayton Corp.
Coca Cola Bottling Co. of
St. Louis (Del.)
Consolidated Dearborn Corp.
Curlee Clothing Co.

Appendix 7

Day-Brite Lighting Co.
Dewey Portland Cement Co.

Epsco, Inc.

Fifteen Oil Co.
Fluid Power Pump Co.
Four Star Television Co.
Fox-Stanley Photo Products
Funsten (R. E.) Co.

Gem International, Inc.
General Battery & Ceramic Corp. (Pa.)

Henry's Drive-In, Inc.
Hirsch (P. N.) & Co.
Honeggers' & Co., Inc.
Howell Instruments, Inc.
Hydraulic-Press Brick Co.

Infotronics Corp.
International Super Stores, Inc.

Jackes-Evans Manufacturing Co.

Kearney-National, Inc.

Laclede Steel Co.
Linco International, Inc.
Londontown Manufacturing Co.
Long Mile Rubber Corp.

McWood Corp.
Mallinckrodt Chemical Works
Metal Goods Corp.
Mexico Refractories Co.
Mid-States Business Capital Corp.
   (Mo.)
Midwest Rubber Reclaiming Co.
Mississippi Glass Co.
Mississippi River Transmission Corp.
Mississippi Valley Helicopters, Inc.
   (Mo.)
Missouri Natural Gas
Missouri Pacific Railroad Co.
Missouri Research Laboratories, Inc.

National Oats Co.

Obear-Nester Glass Co.
Olin Oil & Gas Corp.
Ozark Corp.

Parkview Drugs, Inc.

Precision Automotive Components Co.
Progressive Industries Corp.

R. C. Can Co.
Ralston Purina Co.
Reardon Co.
Rentex Services Corp.

Sage International, Inc.
St. Louis Shipbuilding & Steel Co.
St. Louis Steel Castings, Inc.
Scruggs-Vandervoort-Barney, Inc.
Seven-Up Bottling Co. (St. Louis, Mo.)
Stainless Steel Products, Inc.
Steak 'n Shake, Inc. (Del.)

Texas Capital Corp.
Trenton Foods, Inc.
Tyson's Foods, Inc.

University Computing Co.

Velvet Freeze, Inc. (St. Louis, Mo.)
Viking Freight Co.

Walston Aviation, Inc.
Wetterau Foods, Inc.
White (Martha) Foods, Inc.
White-Rodgers Co.
World Color Press, Inc.
Wrather Corp.

SAN FRANCISCO

Addison-Wesley Publishing Co., Inc.
Allied Properties
American Factors Ltd.
American Forest Products Corp.
American President Lines Ltd. (Del.)
American Recreation Centers, Inc.
Ampex Corp.
Applied Magnetics Corp.
Applied Physics Corp.
Applied Technology, Inc.
Aristocrat Travel Products
Arizona Bancorporation

Babcock Electronics Corp.
Barnes-Hind Pharmaceuticals, Inc.
Bekins Van & Storage Co.
Big "C" Stores, Inc.
Boise Cascade Corp.
Boothe Leasing Corp.

99

Returns in OTC Stock Markets

Boston Capital Corp.
Bruener (John) Co.
Brunswig Drug Co.
Bullocks, Inc.

California Financial Corp.
California Interstate Telephone Co.
California Liquid Gas Corp.
California Portland Cement Co.
California Water Service Co.
California Water & Telephone Co.
California-Pacific Utilities Co.
Capital Funding Corp.
Chemical Process Co.
Chicago Aerial Industries, Inc.
Coleman Engineering Co.
Consolidated Freightways, Inc. (Del.)
Crown-Bremson Industries, Inc.
Cyclotron Corp.
Cyprus Mines Corp.

Dashew Business Machines, Inc.
Data Design Laboratories (Calif.)
Del Monte Properties Co.
Dialaphone (Calif.)
Dickson Electronics Corp.
Dole (James) Engineering Co.
Ducommun Metals and Supply Co.
Dutron Corp.
Dymo Industries, Inc.

ESD Co.
Eichler Homes, Inc.
Eitel-McCullough, Inc.
Elmar Electronics, Inc.

First Bancorporation
First Security Corp. (Ogden, Utah)
Fluor Corp.
Fritzi of California Manufacturing
   Corp. (Calif.)

General Brewing Corp.
General Recorded Tape, Inc.
Geothermal Resources International,
   Inc.
Gerber Products Co.
Gertsch Products, Inc.
Granger Associates (Calif.)
Guardian Paper Co.

Hewlett-Packard Co.
Hexcel Products, Inc.
Hotel Equities Corp.

Hyster Co.

International Electronic Research Corp.
International Rectifier Corp.
Interstate Hosts, Inc.

Jorgensen (Earle M.) Co.

Kellogg Co.
Kingsburg Cotton Oil Co.

Langendorf United Bakeries, Inc.
   (Del.)
Le Gran Corp. (Calif.)
Lightcraft-General (Calif.)
Lilli Ann Corp.
Lockhart Corp.
Lucky Lager Brewing Co.
Lucky Stores, Inc.

Macco Corp. of California
McCormick Selph Associates, Inc.
Magnin (Joseph) Co., Inc.
Mark Systems, Inc.
Mayfair Markets
Melabs Co.
Meyer (Fred), Inc.
Microwave Electronics Corp.
Mohawk Petroleum Corp.
Monogram Precision Industries, Inc.
Morrison-Knudsen Co., Inc.

Nalley's, Inc.
National Motor Bearing Co., Inc.
Newell Associates (Calif.)
Norris-Thermador Corp.

Optical Coating Laboratory
Oregon Metallurgical Corp.

Pacific Air Lines, Inc.
Pacific Coast Holdings, Inc.
Pacific Delta Gas, Inc.
Pacific Far East Line, Inc.
Pacific Gas Transmission Co.
Pacific Intermountain Express Co.
Pacific Plantronics, Inc.
Pacific Vegetable Oil Corp.
Packard-Bell Co.
Pepsi-Cola United Bottlers, Inc.
Permanente Cement Co.
Premier Corp. of America
Products Research Co. (Calif.)
Purex Corp. Ltd.

Appendix 7

Purity Stores Ltd.

Redcor Corp.
Regan Industries, Inc. (Calif.)
Research Specialties Co.
Revell, Inc. (Calif.)
Roddis Plywood Corp.
Roos Atkins
Royal Industries, Inc.

San Francisco & Oakland Helicopter
    Airlines, Inc.
San Jose Water Works
Sawyer's, Inc.
See's Candy Shops, Inc. (Calif.)
Siegler Corp.
Simon Stores, Inc.
Skaggs Drug Centers, Inc.
Skymark Airlines, Inc.
Southern California Water Co.
Southern Nevada Power Co.
Space Ordnance Systems, Inc.
Stater Brothers Markets
Stecher-Traung-Schmidt Corp.
Stuart Co.
Subscription Television, Inc.
Super Mold Corp.

Telephone Utilities, Inc. (Wash.)
Thermal Power Co.
Thrifty Drug Stores Co., Inc.
Tinsley Laboratories, Inc.

Tool Research & Engineering Corp.
Torque Controls Corp.
Trans International Airlines Corp.
Tronchemics Research, Inc.

URS Systems Corp.
Ultex Corp.
United Control Corp.
United Electrodynamics, Inc.
U.S. Leasing & Discount Corp.
Urethane Corp. of California
Utah Southern Oil Co.

Vacu-Dry Co.
Van Camp Sea Food Co., Inc.
Van Waters and Rogers, Inc.
Vangas, Inc.
Varadyne Industries
Varian Associates
Varner-Ward Leasing
Viking Industries, Inc.

Wayne Manufacturing Co.
West Coast Telephone Co. (Wash.)
Westcoast Transmission Co. Ltd.
Western Gear Corp.
Western Microwave Laboratories
Western Utilities Corp.
Whittaker Corp.

Yuba Industries, Inc.

Index

Index

Acquisition: of company by closely held company, 7

Aggregate regional OTC market: explained, 36–37; one-year portfolio returns from, 37–39, 43, 85; and highest-return stocks, 56; and market risk, 60; Betas of, 67–70

American Stock Exchange, 3, 75

Archer, Stephen H., 60n, 62

Arditti, Fred D., 51n

Asked price: described, 8–9; and calculation of rate of return, 20; as used in study, 21

Atlanta Constitution, 8

Atlanta OTC market, 7, 36, 79: growth of number of stocks in, 11; assessment of portfolio returns from, 39–43; proportion of highest-return stocks from, 56; proportion of lowest-return stocks from, 58; market value of stocks in, 73, 86; median bid price for stocks in, 74; number of stocks in portfolios from, 86; stocks studied from, 93–94

Bankruptcy, 7, 74

Banks, 5, 7n, 10n, 11n: Betas for portfolios of trust funds of, 67n

Beta coefficients: defined, 66–67; of institutional portfolios, 67; of OTC portfolios relative to NYSE portfolios, 67–69

Beta measures: illustration of calculation of, 65–67; of OTC portfolios relative to NYSE portfolios, 67–70, 80; instability of, 69–70, 80

Bid price: described, 8–9; and calculation of rate of return, 20; as used in study, 21; for OTC stocks for selected years, 74

Bonds, 3

"Capital Asset Prices: A Theory of Market Equilibrium under Conditions of Risk," 59n

Capital changes, 11, 65: defined, 8; and rate-of-return measures, 18–19, 21

Cash distribution: defined, 8

Cash receipts, 21

Cash sale, 74

Center for Research in Securities Prices at the University of Chicago, 25

Chicago Daily News, 8

Chicago OTC market, 7, 36, 79: growth of number of stocks in, 11; assessment of portfolio returns from, 39–43; proportion of highest-return stocks from, 56; proportion of lowest-return stocks from, 58; market value of stocks in, 73, 86; median bid price for stocks in, 74; number of stocks in portfolios from, 86; stocks studied from, 94–96

Common stocks: requirements for listing of, on exchanges, 3–4, 74; included in study, 3, 7–9, 87–101; eligibility of, for OTC trading, 4; transition process in market quotation of, 6–7, 74–76; mentioned, *passim. See also* National OTC market, NYSE, Regional OTC market

Companies: inter-market movement of stocks of, 6–7, 74–76; included in study, 87–101

Control Data Corporation: used as illustration, 6, 9

Data bank: constructed for stocks in study, 8, 11; accuracy of, 9

Dice, Charles A., 16n

Returns in OTC Stock Markets

Diversification: and mutual funds, 59n; reduction of risk by, 59–62; purpose of, 60; two methods of, 60; as reason for investment in OTC markets, 82
"Diversification and the Reduction of Dispersion: An Empirical Analysis," 60n, 62n
Dividends, 15, 76: as part of data bank, 8, 11; as capital change, 11; NQB Index stocks paying cash, 18; and rate-of-return measures, 18–21, 65; NYSE stocks paying cash, 18, 71–72; OTC stocks paying cash, 18, 71–72; assumed investor strategy concerning, 21, 22
Dow Jones Composite Average, 15
Dow Jones Utility Average, 15

Eastern OTC market, 10, 76
Eiteman, David K., 16n
Eiteman, Wilford J., 16n
Evans, John L., 60n, 62

Federal Reserve Banks, 7, 36
Fisher, Lawrence: time period of studies by, 25, 27, 39n, 55n; basis of studies by, 25, 28n; data from studies by, compared with OTC market data, 27–31, 33–34, 39, 48, 53, 55, 67–69; treatment of transaction costs in studies by, 34n; on diversification, 62

High-return portfolios: defined, 47, 49; compared across markets, 47–49, 80; achievement of, 50–51
High-return stocks: defined, 54; magnitude of, compared across markets, 54–55; frequency of, compared across markets, 54–55, 57, 58. See also Highest-return stocks
Highest-return portfolios: skewness of, 50–51; defined, 55–56. See also High-return portfolios
Highest-return stocks: defined, 55–56; compared across markets, 55–56; in individual regional markets, 56. See also High-return stocks

Income tax, 22
Indexes: for NYSE, 15, 16, 24, 62n, 66; for OTC market, 15–18, 23–24, 72n, 79, 80; use of, 15, 23–24, 65, 71, 72n, 79, 80
Institutional portfolios: typical Betas of, 67

Insurance companies, 7n, 10n, 11n: Betas for portfolios of, 67n
Investment Company Act of 1940, 59n
Investor strategy: assumed in study, 21–22, 24–25, 80; and participation in OTC markets, 81–82

Jessup, Paul F., 43n, 81n

Liquidation: of company, 7, 74
Long-run returns: from portfolios compared with one-year returns, 31–32; from national OTC portfolios, 31–34; from national OTC portfolios compared with NYSE portfolios, 33–34; impact of transaction costs on, 34n; from regional OTC portfolios, 43; and cross-market comparison of high-return stocks, 55; and cross-market comparison of low-return stocks, 57
Lorie, James H.: time period of studies by, 25, 27, 39n, 55n; basis of studies by, 25, 28n; data from studies by, compared with OTC data, 27–31, 33–34, 39, 48, 53, 55, 67–69; treatment of transaction costs in studies by, 34n; on diversification, 62
Low-return portfolios: defined, 47, 52; compared across markets, 51–53, 80–81
Low-return stocks: defined, 54, 57; compared across markets, 57, 58, 80–81
Lowest-return portfolios: defined, 53; skewness of, 53. See also Low-return portfolios
Lowest-return stocks: defined, 57; compared across markets, 57–58; in individual regional markets, 58. See also Low-return stocks

Market portfolio: defined, 66; used in calculating Betas, 66–67
Market quotations: in Wall Street Journal, 4–5, 6, 8, 10; in regional newspapers, 4–6, 8; of OTC stocks, 4–11 passim, 74–75; reasons for termination of, 6–7, 11, 74–75; for stocks used in study, 8–9; reliability of, 9; overlap of, 11
Market risk: defined, 59n; effect of diversification on, 59–60; stability of, 60, 62; for OTC markets, 60–62, 80

Index

Market value: of OTC stocks, 17, 72–74, 76, 86–87; of NYSE stocks, 17, 73; calculation of, 72, 74

Mergers: and transition of stocks to new market, 6–7, 76; as capital change, 8

Minneapolis-St. Paul OTC market, 6, 7, 36, 79: growth of number of stocks in, 11; assessment of portfolio returns from, 39–43; proportion of highest-return stocks from, 56; proportion of lowest-return stocks from, 58; market value of stocks in, 73, 86; median bid price for stocks in, 74; number of stocks in portfolios from, 86; stocks studied from, 96–98

Minneapolis Tribune, 8

Mokkelbost, Per B., 60n, 62n

Mutual funds, 81: and diversification, 59n; Betas for portfolios of, 67n

National Association of Securities Dealers (NASD): and classification of OTC stocks, 4–5, 6, 11; and validity of OTC market quotations, 9

National Association of Securities Dealers Automated Quotation system (NASDAQ), 4n, 15n

National Quotation Bureau: daily quotation sheets of, 4

NQB Index. *See* National Quotation Bureau (NQB) OTC Industrial Index

National Quotation Bureau (NQB) OTC Industrial Index: described, 15–16; list of stocks in, 16; representativeness of, 16–18, 23, 72n, 79, 80; computation of, 16, 24; compared to rate-of-return measures, 23–24

National OTC market: as judged by NASD, 4; quotation of stocks in, 4–5, 6, 8, 10–11; relation to other OTC markets, 5, 6–7, 74–76; stocks studied from, 8, 10–11, 87–93; composition of portfolios of, 8, 23n, 26–27, 31, 32, 42n, 48, 49, 52, 67n; increase of stocks in, 9–10; index of stocks in, 15–18, 23–24, 72n, 79, 80; market value of stocks in, 17, 72–74, 76, 87; price and dividend characteristics of, 18; stocks paying cash dividends, 18, 71–72, 76; *1969* rate of return from representative portfolio of, 22–24; one-year portfolio returns in, 22–24, 26–31, 34–35, 37–40, 42–43, 85; one-year portfolio returns compared with NYSE, 27–31, 34–35; long-run portfolio returns from, 31–35; long-run portfolio returns compared with NYSE, 33–35; one-year portfolio returns compared with regional OTC markets, 37–40, 42–43; high-return portfolios compared with other markets, 47–49, 80; skewness of highest-return portfolios from, 50–51, 53; low-return portfolios compared with other markets, 51–53, 80; skewness of lowest-return portfolios from, 53; highest-return stocks compared with other markets, 55–56; high-return stocks compared with other markets, 55, 57, 58, 80; low-return stocks compared with other markets, 57, 58, 80; lowest-return stocks compared with other markets, 58; and unsystematic risk, 60–62; and market risk, 60–62, 80; Beta coefficients of, 67–70; stability of Betas of, 69–70; bid price for stocks in, 74; mentioned, *passim*

New York Stock Exchange (NYSE): described, 3–4; listing criteria of, 3, 74; transition of OTC stocks to, 6, 75; increase of stocks in, 9–10; indexes of, 15, 16, 24, 62n, 66; market value of stocks in, 17, 72–74; price and dividend characteristics of stocks in, 18; stocks paying cash dividends, 18, 71–72; studies of, 25, 27–28, 39n, 55n, 62; composition of portfolios from, used in study, 27–28; one-year portfolio returns compared with national OTC market, 27–31, 34–35, 80; long-run portfolio returns compared with national OTC market, 33–35; one-year portfolio returns compared with regional OTC markets, 39, 43, 80; high-return portfolios compared with other markets, 48; low-return portfolios compared with other markets, 53, 80; high-return stocks compared with other markets, 55, 58, 80; low-return stocks compared with other markets, 57, 80; and unsystematic risk, 62; Beta coefficients of, compared to OTC markets, 67–70, 80

New York Stock Exchange Composite Indicator, 15

Index

"Risk and the Required Return on Equity," 51n
"Risk-Return Relationships in Regional Securities Markets," 43n, 81n

St. Louis OTC market, 7, 79: growth of number of stocks in, 11; unavailability of data for, 36; assessment of portfolio returns from, 39–43; proportion of highest-return stocks from, 56; proportion of lowest-return stocks from, 58; market value of stocks in, 73, 86; median bid price for stocks in, 74; number of stocks in portfolios from, 86; stocks studied from, 98–99
St. Louis Post-Dispatch, 8
San Francisco Chronicle, 8
San Francisco OTC market, 7, 36, 79: growth of number of stocks in, 11; assessment of portfolio returns from, 39–43; proportion of highest-return stocks from, 56; proportion of lowest-return stocks from, 58; market value of stocks in, 73, 86; median bid price for stocks in, 74; number of stocks in portfolios from, 86; stocks studied from, 99–101
Securities and Exchange Commission: exchanges registered with, 3; and price quotations, 9
Securities Exchange Act of *1934*, 3
Sharpe, William F., 59n
Short-run returns: from national OTC portfolios, 26–31, 34–35, 80, 85; from national OTC portfolios compared with NYSE portfolios, 27–31, 34–35; from portfolios compared with long-run returns, 31–34; impact of transaction costs on, 34n; from regional OTC portfolios, 37–43, 80, 85; and cross-market comparison of high-return stocks, 55; and cross-market comparison of low-return stocks, 57
Skewness: implications of, 47, 51, 53; within highest-return OTC portfolios, 50–51, 53; within lowest-return OTC portfolios, 53
"Some Studies of Variability of Returns on Investments in Common Stocks," 30, 33: basis of, 28n; time period for, 39n; and availability of data on NYSE stocks, 55n; and diversification by portfolio size, 62

Spread, 9
Standard & Poor's 500 Stock Index, 15, 62n, 66
Standard Statistics Compustat Tape, 62n
Stock Market, The, 16n
Stock split: and rate of return, 18–19, 21
Stocks. *See* Common stocks
Study: markets examined in, 3, 4, 7–8; specifications for, 3, 7–12, 79; time period of, 7; composition of portfolios for, 8, 23n, 26–28, 31, 32, 36–37, 42n, 48, 49, 52, 67n; investor strategy assumed by, 21–22, 24–25, 80; data from, compared with Fisher and Lorie studies, 25, 27–31, 33–34, 39, 48, 53, 55, 62, 67–69; risk measure used in, 60n; summarized conclusions of, 79–82; names of OTC stocks used in, 87–101
Systematic risk. *See* Market risk

Transaction costs, 9, 22, 24, 80: impact of, on portfolio returns, 34–35
Transient OTC investor hypothesis, 81

Unsystematic risk: defined, 59; effect of diversification on, 59–62; and OTC markets, 59–62, 80; stability of, 60, 62; and NYSE, 62
"Unsystematic Risk over Time," 62n
Upson, Roger B., 43n, 81n

Value. *See* Market value, Rate-of-return measures
Volatility, relative: as measurable risk concept, 65; defined, 65; illustration of measurement of, 65–67; of NYSE stocks, 67–69, 80; of OTC stocks, 67–70, 80; stability of, 69–70, 80; effect of payment of cash dividends on, 71

Wall Street Journal: OTC quotations in, 4–5, 6, 8, 10–11; used to define population for study, 8, 10–11; "Over-the-Counter Market" list of, 10; "National Market" list of, 10; NQB Index reported in, 16
Warrants, 3
Weekly OTC market: as judged by NASD, 4–5; overlap with regional OTC market, 5

109